On Living

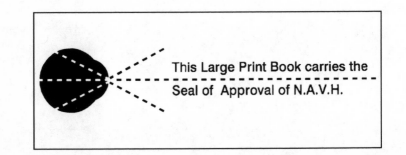

This Large Print Book carries the
Seal of Approval of N.A.V.H.

ON LIVING

KERRY EGAN

THORNDIKE PRESS
A part of Gale, Cengage Learning

GALE
CENGAGE Learning·

Farmington Hills, Mich • San Francisco • New York • Waterville, Maine
Meriden, Conn • Mason, Ohio • Chicago

GALE
CENGAGE Learning®

LIBRARY OF CONGRESS CATALOGING-IN-PUBLICATION DATA

Names: Egan, Kerry, author.
Title: On living / by Kerry Egan.
Description: Large Print edition. | Waterville : Thorndike Press, 2017. | Series: Thorndike Press Large Print inspirational
Identifiers: LCCN 2016042664| ISBN 9781410495945 (hardcover) | ISBN 1410495949 (hardcover)
Subjects: LCSH: Conduct of life. | Life. | Death. | Spiritual life. | Terminally ill. | Church work with the terminally ill. | Large type books.
Classification: LCC BJ1589 .E395 2017 | DDC 170/.44—dc23
LC record available at https://lccn.loc.gov/2016042664

Published in 2017 by arrangement with Riverhead Books, an imprint of Penguin Publishing Group, a division of Penguin Random House LLC *for my children*

CONTENTS

The Stories We Tell

"I never did become wise. Y'always think that when you get old, you're supposed to become wise. But here I am, fixin' to die, and I never did."

Gloria's milky blue eyes widened and she raised her eyebrows. She laughed, just a little bit.

"I'd have thought, with all I been through, that if anyone might could figure it all out before it was too late, it was me." She laughed again, a sort of rolling chuckle that interrupted her slow, drawling cadence. She laughed all the time.

"You know." She leaned toward me and sunlight lit up the white baby fuzz on top of her head. "I always wished I could meet a writer, and tell him my stories, so other people could hear them and not make the same mistakes I made. I'd just give him my stories. I'd say, 'Here, take them and tell them.' And you know what crazy stories I've

9

got. But I never did. I never did meet a writer."

I was uncertain what to say. I had once written a book, more than ten years before, but I wasn't here as a writer now. Gloria was a hospice patient and I was her chaplain. I couldn't remember if I'd ever told her about my past, but I didn't think I had.

"I used to pray for it all the time, that I might could meet someone," she continued. "But I guess that prayer won't ever be answered now."

We fell silent, and I hoped Gloria would change the subject.

She lifted her hands from the armrests and let them fall as she sighed heavily. "I never even leave this house. I'm stuck here. How could I ever meet a real writer now?"

She looked at me, shook her head, and smiled.

"I prayed and prayed and prayed. Some prayers just don't get answered, I suppose." She laughed, but this time it sounded sad.

It was getting ridiculous. I hesitated for one more silent minute, then said, "Gloria, did I ever tell you I was once a writer?"

"A real writer?" Her sparse eyebrows flew up again.

"Yes, but it was a long time ago."

"Like someone who wrote a book?"

"Yes. Published and everything."

She threw up her hands and looked at the ceiling. "All this time I've been waiting for a man, Jesus!" she yelled. She bounced just slightly in her recliner. She turned and looked at me. "I thought you'd be a man, Kerry! But this is it!" She rocked back and forth and spread her arms wide. "I can feel it! This is the answer. The Holy Spirit sent you to me, and I've already told you all my stories. Now you've just got to go write them down. Maybe they could help someone. Maybe someone else can get wise from them. Promise me you'll tell my stories."

While a few patients before Gloria had told me that they wished other people could learn from their life stories — had even given me permission to share their stories with others — it was Gloria and the promise I made to her that led to this little book. I had been holding on to patients' stories for many years by then, the stories that patients had poured out and puzzled over, the stories they turned over in their minds like the rosary beads and worn Bibles they turned over in their hands. I hoarded them, locked them away in my heart.

Often, but not always, my patients found some measure of peace as we talked. Often, but not always, their faith in something good and greater than themselves was affirmed. Often, but not always, they found strength they didn't know they had to make amends with the people in their lives, and courage to move forward without fear toward their deaths. Always, they taught me something.

We all have some experiences that we hold up as the stories that define our lives. Patients told me those stories, sometimes once or twice, and sometimes dozens of times over. Usually the way they told them changed with each telling. Not the basics of the story, but what they emphasized, the details, the connections they made between the details, and eventually, the connections they made between the various stories, even if the events they recounted happened decades apart. The meaning they found in their stories expanded and shifted.

Almost always, their stories were about shame or grief or trauma: My child died in my arms when he was four. My wife left me for another man while I was a soldier far away. I killed someone. My father raped me. I drank my life away. My husband beat my children and I did nothing to stop it because I was afraid. I was not loved, and I don't know why. The stories confused them. How could these things possibly have happened, and what did it all mean?

I don't know if listening to other people's life stories as they die can make you wise, but I do know that it can heal your soul. I know this because those stories healed mine.

Just as was true for every one of my patients, something had happened to me, too. What I thought of as the story that had shaped my life up to that point was one I was ashamed of. I thought I was broken and cracked and could not be put back together again, that I was destroyed at the very deepest part of me, and that this was something that could never be made better. When I started working in hospice, I didn't yet understand that everyone — everyone — is broken and cracked.

Just a few months after starting to work in hospice, I walked into the dark, run-down room of a nursing home patient whose chart said she had both colon cancer and advanced dementia. Instead of the weak, curled-up patient I expected, I found a beautiful woman with tightly set white curls on her head sitting ramrod straight on her bed. She was like an emaciated, blue-tinged china doll on the expanse of white institutional sheets.

Instead of greeting me with the deep silence of end-stage dementia, she spoke in a broad New England accent about what it was like to lose pieces of your body, pieces you had never appreciated until they were gone. It can happen, even with end-stage dementia, that a patient will have moments, or even a day, of perfect clarity. As she talked about her many years of treatment for cancer, a pink flush crept up the papery skin of her neck and across her face. First her hands and then her whole body quivered. Her voice slowly got louder as her body got tenser.

"I have no asshole!" she finally exploded. Her tiny white fists hit the bed in unison. Even using all her strength, she barely dented the sheets. "I can't shit!"

She looked away and stared at the radiator intently. When she spoke again, her voice was a gravelly whisper. "Every person who came in that hospital room, they all stared down at me. They didn't actually see me. They didn't want to see me. They talked to me in baby talk like I'm an idiot. They looked at me and thought, 'I'm happy I'm not like her.' Even if they were nice, I knew they thanked God that they weren't me. I knew they only saw a crazy, pathetic old woman who doesn't even have an asshole."

We sat in silence for a few seconds that felt like minutes. When she looked at me again, I said, "What you needed was compassion, but what you got was pity."

"Yes." She sucked in air. "Yes, that's right. That's exactly right." She looked at me with surprise. She furrowed her eyebrows and said in a different voice, an almost-accusing voice, "You're very young."

"I'm older than I look."

"No. You're young," she said flatly. "How do you know these things?"

"Well." I wasn't expecting that question. "Well, I've been through some hard things. I know what pity feels like."

She sat up even straighter and pinned me with her eyes. "Why? What's your story? What happened to you?"

I could feel heat prickle through my body. "I'd rather not say, because I'm here to talk about your life. My role as the hospice chaplain is to listen to you, to help you draw on your spiritual strengths to get through this time." I tried to sound professional.

"You're ashamed."

"No, no. Not at all." Suddenly I wanted to stand up and run. I could hear the ocean in my ears and feel my heart in my chest. I held on to the edge of the bed. "It's just that I know myself, and I know that if I start to talk about me, that's all I'll talk about, and that's not right, because I'm here to visit you and listen to you and not me. It's just not something I should talk about."

I was lying, of course. I was ashamed, and she knew it. But she was also kind enough not to call me on it.

Her brown eyes, bulging slightly from her bony eye sockets and sunken cheeks, stared into me. Then she reached for my hands and cleared her throat.

"Whatever bad things have happened to you in your life, whatever hard things you've gone through, you have to do three things: You have to accept it. You have to be kind to it," she said slowly, squeezing my fingers together. "And listen to me. You have to let it be kind to you."

I didn't understand what she meant. I didn't know how to let my hard thing be kind to me.

I had an emergency C-section with my first baby. During the surgery, the epidural anesthesia failed. I could feel everything, but the dangerous part was that I was moving while I was still cut open. The emergency anesthesia I was given is called ketamine, a drug usually used only on horses, on battlefields, and at raves. It doesn't work the way a typical anesthetic does, by shutting off the body's ability to feel pain. Instead, it works as a "dissociative anesthesia" — that is, by severing the mind-body connection so that you do not recognize pain as such. In other words, it triggers a psychotic state.

In my unlucky and unusual case, the state wasn't temporary. That drug-induced psychotic disorder lasted seven months. As a new mother I was suddenly plunged into a world of hallucinations, delusions, dissociation, suicidal ideation, and catatonia. I have almost no memories of my son's first half year of life, and I slept through the next eighteen months on a cocktail of powerful psychiatric medications. I got better, with the help of lots of therapy, drugs, and time. But I lost years of my life to that psychosis.

And I was still deeply ashamed that I had lost my mind.

I went back to see that dementia patient many times, always hoping, selfishly, to have another conversation. I wanted to learn what she'd meant, how she let the bad things that had happened be kind to her. But she never spoke a single word again. She couldn't even make or maintain eye contact. She lay in bed or in one of the huge padded vinyl recliners on wheels that nursing homes use for patients who have no control over their bodies. The dementia swallowed her back up. Only a curled-up and constricted body and a glazed silence remained.

I would sit with her and sing to her, hold her hands if they didn't look painfully clenched. I don't know if it gave her any comfort at all. A few months later she died, alone in her dark room in the middle of the night.

She likely had no memory of ever meeting me, but I've been holding on to and thinking about what she said ever since. About the wisdom to be found in stories like hers, and the kindness to be found even in our hardest things, even now, in the midst of living.

"Mommy." My five-year-old son sighed deeply and looked at the box of applesauce cups on the counter. He grabbed both my hands as I tried to make school lunches before work. "My have an idea." This was always his opening gambit. "I know you need to go to work to make people die, but I really want to go to Friendly's today." He smiled and nodded. "So? Mommy? Can we go to Friendly's? For lunch? And ice cream? A make-your-own sundae? With gummy bears and rainbow sprinkles? You love Friendly's! Yeah?"

"Wait wait wait!" I said.

He smiled a kindergarten smile, all gums and no teeth, and kept nodding his head.

"Back up. What do you think I do at work?"

"Make people die so they can go to Heaven," he said matter-of-factly. "But you can do that tomorrow and today we can go to Friendly's? Right? You love ice cream, too. You love it more than me. More than anybody. So let's go to Friendly's. People can die tomorrow." He nodded some more.

He seemed remarkably calm that his mother was a Grim Reaper in clogs and pants that were always too snug in the waist, holding the power over life and death in the same hands that held his applesauce cup.

For the record, I don't make people die.

But I can't fault my son for not understanding what his mother did at work. Most people don't really know what chaplains do. Sometimes even other hospice workers have only a vague inkling, usually involving holding hands and saying the Hail Mary.

I've had a hard time explaining it to others myself.

"So I'm a little confused," a woman at a book club meeting once asked as we stood next to a tray of cheese and grapes. "What does a chaplain actually do?"

"We're part of the hospice team, and our role is to offer spiritual care and support to patients, families, and staff," I said, my standard response, as I piled my plate with crackers and that delicious herb-crusted goat cheese you only get to eat at parties.

"That means nothing to me," she replied. I ate a cracker. She tried again. "So tell me exactly what you did today at work."

That day, I had been at a nursing home and had visited half a dozen indigent patients with end-stage dementia and no families.

People with end-stage dementia are both the easiest and the hardest patients of all for a hospice chaplain. Like that porcelain doll patient, they sit, their tiny bodies curled and twisted in painful muscle contractions, in those huge padded recliners on wheels, with stuffed animals to comfort them. Their eyes, now enormous in sunken sockets, stare into the distance. Crusts form at the corners of their open mouths. Their skin tears like a wet tissue. They cannot speak, or walk, or feed themselves. In the last weeks or months — in a few of the saddest situations I've seen, even for long, lingering years before they finally die — they can no longer smile or hold up their heads.

How do you give spiritual care to this person? What can you offer when you don't know whether a prayer, or a song, even the touch of a hand would be comforting or upsetting? When the person can't tell you who they are, and there are no family or friends to tell you a little bit about them?

Imagine being in their place. Some stranger shows up in your room. You can't tell her to leave if you want to be alone. You can't ask her to stay if you are lonely or afraid. You can't ask her to please stop talking, or to please stay and keep singing. You can't tell her to stop reading from the Bible if you're Buddhist, or saying a prayer if you're atheist. You can't ask her to say a decade of the Rosary if that's the only thing that brings you comfort. You can't tell this strange lady that her hand lightly on your wrist is causing excruciating pain — or that all you want is the warmth and softness of human touch, and you're wondering why she won't hold your hand.

Imagine being the chaplain with such a stranger, and not knowing whether what you do or do not do causes comfort or pain. After emerging from a day spent with half a dozen such patients — what a colleague once called "the Wall of Dementia" — how could I explain what I did?

But something in me wanted to try. Few people ever asked about my work, and that could be lonely.

I said that on that particular day, I sat with my patients. I looked to see whether they seemed comfortable, and if they didn't, I talked to the nurse or aide. I might have gently touched their hands or arms if it seemed to relax them. I might have sung to them. I might have picked up and shown them the photographs and objects on their dressers, if there were any. But mostly, I just did the most basic, and the most difficult, work of a chaplain: I tried to be present.

"So you just sat there?"

"No. Well, yes. I mean, I sat there, but I didn't just sit there."

She raised an eyebrow.

"I sat with them and offered a peaceful presence."

"A peaceful presence? And exactly how do you do that? You make it sound like you're offering coffee."

Now was the moment when I could just smile warmly and change the subject. The cheese tempted me. I could get back to it in earnest if I just made a quick, amusing comment that shut down the whole discussion. Or I could push on and attempt to explain, knowing I would likely sound ridiculous to her.

"Well." I took a deep breath as I turned to face her again. "I take a deep breath before I enter the room, and I ask God for help. I remind myself why I'm there, and I let go of everything else in my mind. I try to focus love in my heart. Then I go in and say hello, and notice if the person notices me. Then I smile, but not too big a smile, and I tell them my name. I try to create a feeling of peace and acceptance and love with how I move and sit and look. I focus all my energy on their face."

The look on her face passed from skepticism to incredulity. But I've never shied away from publicly embarrassing myself, and so I finished with "And then I imagine a giant bubble of love encompassing the patient and me. That's my process. That's how I try to create a peaceful presence. But I'm sure other chaplains do it differently."

She was silent for a good ten seconds. Long enough to make the silence uncomfortable.

"So you just sit there and try to love them? Is that what you're saying?" she said coolly. "This is a real job? That people go to graduate school for?"

"Well, there's usually a lot more to it than

that," I said.

"But that's what you did today? All day? And you got paid for it?"

"Yup."

"You consider this work?"

What really cut to the quick is that on a day like that, up against the Wall of Dementia, I, too, questioned what I did all day.

In the movie version of hospice chaplaincy, the one most people seem to believe, I'd swoop in minutes before death to hear a patient's whispered confession, while consoling the wailing family. The patient would gasp some final beautiful words, and then suddenly, quietly, peacefully stop breathing. I'd solemnly close his eyes by passing my hand slowly over his face.

It sounds good, but it's fiction. Most of a chaplain's work in hospice — what we call spiritual care — happens in pockets of time weeks, months, and, in some unusual cases, even years before the patient dies. I can count on my hands and feet the number of hospice patients' deaths I have actually witnessed. In fact, I've been present at more deaths as a chaplain at a hospital than in hospice.

Some people, often skeptics or those who have been hurt by religion in the past, like the woman at my book club, assume that chaplains are charlatans, or proselytizers intent on foisting our beliefs on vulnerable patients and grieving families. Maybe there are some chaplains like that, but I've never met one. Some chaplains are more skillful and empathic than others, but I've never met one I've considered an asshole.

But what we do is hard to describe. The essence of any meaningful spiritual care is, by its nature, nebulous and ineffable, and trying to describe it tends to make you sound silly.

It would have been easier to explain what I did that night at book club if I'd spent any part of the day with a patient or family who could communicate, and with whom I already had a relationship, and who wanted to talk. Because in that case, I could have explained that hospice chaplains are sort of the opposite of storytellers. We're story holders.

We listen to the stories that people believe have shaped their lives. We listen to the stories people choose to tell, and the meaning they make of those stories.

While religion plays a central role in spiritual care for many patients, it doesn't for many others. Spiritual care, faith, and religion are not the same thing. Some chaplains might also be priests and pastors, but in their roles as chaplains, they don't preach or teach.

Instead, they create a space — a sacred time and place — in which people can look at the lives they've led and try to figure out what it all means to them.

When you talk to hundreds of people who are dying and looking back over their lives, you come to realize something startling: Every single person out there has a crazy story. Every single person has some bizarre, life-shattering, pull-the-rug-out-from-under-you story in their past, or will experience one in their future. Every shopper in the grocery store, every telemarketer on the phone, every mother at school pickup, every banker striding down the sidewalk. Money, faith, popularity, beauty, power — nothing prevents it.

Every one of us will go through things that destroy our inner compass and pull meaning out from under us. Everyone who does not die young will go through some sort of spiritual crisis, where we have lost our sense of what is right and wrong, possible and impossible, real and not real. Never underestimate how frightening, angering, confusing, devastating it is to be in that place. Making meaning of what is meaningless is hard work. Soul-searching is painful. This process of making or finding meaning at the end of life is what the chaplain facilitates. The chaplain doesn't do the work. The patient does. The chaplain isn't wrestling with the events of a life that don't match up with everything you were taught was true, but she won't turn away in fear, either. She won't try to give you pat answers to get you to stop talking about pain, or shut you down with platitudes that make her feel better but do nothing to resolve the confusion and yearning you feel. A chaplain is not the one laboring to make meaning, but she's been with other people who have. She knows what tends to be helpful, and what doesn't. She might ask questions you would never have considered, or that help you remember other times you survived something hard and other ways you made sense of what seemed senseless. She can reframe the story, and can offer a different interpretation to consider, accept, or reject. She can remind you of the larger story of your life, or the wisdom of your faith tradition. She can hold open a space of prayer or meditation or reflection when you don't have the energy or strength to keep the walls from collapsing. She will not leave you. And maybe most important: She knows the work can be done. She knows you can do it and not crumble into dust.

So many times I've sat in the silence, the air heavy and tense, as a patient searches my face. When you do it often enough, you come to recognize when the moment arrives. There's a feeling of electricity in the air, and the patient tests the charge. This is when I wait, knowing that if I just hold the line, if I wait in silence, no matter how hard that is, somehow, the patient will find the courage. He will say the unspeakable thing. He will admit, not just to himself but to another human being, the thing he thought he could never say, the hard thing he thought would destroy him just by admitting its existence in his life.

But the fact remains that before a chaplain gets to that place with a patient — the place where the patient can stare into a deep hole of meaninglessness, or even leap right into it and wrestle down in the lonely existential muck until a ladder of sorts begins to appear — and somehow, somehow, in ways I still can't fully explain, a ladder always does appear — before all of that, the chaplain has to create a sacred space, and to do that, she has to offer her loving presence first.

Because these stories can be — often are — absolutely terrifying. They were terrifying when they happened, and they are still terrifying. Many people spend a lifetime avoiding these stories, even when these are the stories that shaped them.

So before the patient can bear to dredge them up, he has to know that he is safe to do so. He needs to know he doesn't have to do it alone. And if the chaplain wants to be helpful to the patient as he contemplates taking the leap, she'd better not flinch.

If you think it's not work to stay steady, to remain present, to not pull back in the face of terrible suffering, then you have never been in the face of terrible suffering. It's something I've failed at. I try not to flinch, I try not to be overwhelmed, I try not to run away. But I have.

There are a few patients who haunt me, but the only one I ever dreamed of was the patient I ran away from. I met him when I was a student chaplain in a hospital. He was on a floor the nurses called "Death Valley," a floor for patients who were dependent on ventilators. Most were long-term patients, and most were in a persistent vegetative state. But this young man — barely more than a boy — was not. He was fully awake and fully aware. He was only in the hospital to control an infection, and would then return home. He was not yet twenty.

"He won't stop crying," the nurse said when I found her at the desk, in response to her message on the beeper. "He's been crying for hours. I didn't know what else to do, so I called you."

The patient was broad-shouldered and took up the whole bed. Even with his face swollen from crying, he was startlingly handsome. Between the rhythmic gasps of the ventilator, he told me that he'd been paralyzed from the neck down when he was shot during a robbery on the first day of college, the day after his parents had dropped him off.

"I would have given them my shoes. I would have given them my shoes. I would have given them my shoes. I would have given them my shoes. I would have given them my shoes. I would have given them my shoes," he said over and over to the rhythm of the vent. The speaking valve on his tracheostomy put long, unnatural pauses between his words. He started to cry. His sobs were regulated and controlled by the machine that breathed for him. A wail and then a quiet whir of machinery. But while the sound was regularly, clinically, rhythmically interrupted, his face remained contorted in pain even when no sound could escape. Again and again, wail and whir.

He asked me why God had let this happen. I didn't have an answer. He said no one ever wanted to listen to his story. He asked me to come back to see him again. I said I would. I escaped into the hallway and leaned my back into the cold wall and stared straight ahead, happy to be free.

That was Thursday. I spent Friday finding busywork to do. Then it would be the weekend, and I was counting on him being discharged over the weekend. He was. I never saw him again. I was relieved.

I was frozen at the thought of sitting in the midst of his suffering again. Just the memory of his anguish overwhelmed me. I didn't tell my clinical supervisor of my struggle because I was afraid he would make me go back. I ran away from this boy-man, and I knew he couldn't run after me.

Not flinching is work.

But these aren't the stories anyone wants to hear at a party, when there's goat cheese and crackers in front of you.

It's not that people don't love stories. They do. What do people do when they're at parties? They tell stories, and if it's a great party, they dance. They might drink, and they might even take some drugs, but really, those things are usually the precursors to telling stories.

31

It's stories that heal.

For a long time, I thought my own life experiences marked me as strange and cursed. But after hearing so many stories, I came to realize that I was like everyone else, and that while my experiences might be unique to me, the pain was quite ordinary, and I was not alone in it. That was more healing than anything else.

I have none of the power my kindergarten son believed I did. I don't make people die. People will die whether or not a chaplain visits. We all will.

But my book club acquaintance was wrong, too. There is power in being present with people who are dying. There's power in the stories of their lives and the meanings they found in them. Not the power of life and death, but of healing and wholeness. That power isn't just for those who are dying. It's for anyone who wants to listen.

There are a thousand stories patients have told me, but the ones in this book are the ones people wanted to share. Those patients understood long before I did that some stories are meant to be bundled up and locked away in a chaplain's heart, but some are meant to be told. Their hope, when they said I could share parts of their stories, was that people who still have years, decades, lifetimes left to live would find something in there that could help them learn the things my patients learned so late.

I don't know if these stories will make you wise. But maybe, in seeing that other people have done it, you'll find your own way to let your life be kind to you.

THE CRUCIBLE OF LOVE

When I was a divinity school student and had just started working as a student chaplain at a cancer hospital, a professor asked me about my job. I was twenty-six years old and still learning what a chaplain did.

"I talk to the patients," I told him.

"You talk to patients? Tell me, what do people who are sick and dying talk to the student chaplain about?" he asked.

I hadn't really thought about that before. I tried to quickly run through my memories of what the dozen or so people I'd met with actually talked about. I was really intimidated by this professor and didn't want to look stupid, but all I could come up with was "Mostly we talk about their families."

"Do you talk about God?"

"Umm, not usually."

"Or their religion?"

"Not so much."

"The meaning of their lives?"

"Sometimes."

"And prayer? Do you lead them in prayer? Or ritual?"

"Well." I hesitated. "Sometimes. But not usually, not really."

I felt derision creeping into the professor's voice. "So you just visit people and talk about their families?"

"Well, they talk. I mostly listen."

"Huh." He leaned back in his chair.

A week later, in the middle of a lecture in this professor's crowded class, he started to tell a story about a student he'd once met who was a chaplain intern at a hospital.

"I asked her, 'What exactly do you *do* as a chaplain?' She replied, 'Well, I talk to people about their families.' " He paused for effect. "And *that* was this student's understanding of faith! *That* was as deep as this person's spiritual life went! Talking about other people's families!"

My classmates laughed at the shallow student. The professor was on a roll. "I thought to myself," he continued, "that if I was ever sick in the hospital, if I was ever dying, that the last person I would want to see is some student chaplain wanting to talk to me about my family."

My body went numb with shame. At the time I thought that maybe, if I was a better chaplain, I would know how to talk to people about big spiritual questions. Maybe if dying people met with a good, experienced chaplain, they would talk about God.

Today, more than fifteen years later, if you were to ask me the same question — What do people who are sick and dying talk about with the chaplain? — I would give you the same answer: Mostly, they talk about their families, their mothers and fathers, their sons and daughters.

They talk about the love they felt and the love they gave. Often they talk about the love they didn't receive or the love they didn't know how to offer, or about the love they withheld or maybe never felt for the ones they should have loved unconditionally.

They talk about how they learned what love is, and what it is not. And sometimes, when they are actively dying, fluid gurgling in their throats, they reach out their hands to things I cannot see and they call their parents' names: Mama, Daddy, Mother.

What I didn't understand when I was a student, and what I would explain to that professor now, is that people talk to the chaplain about their families because that is *how* we talk about God. That is *how* we talk about the meaning of our lives. That is *how*

36

we talk about the big spiritual questions of human existence.

We don't live our lives in our heads, in theology and theories. We live our lives in our families: the families we are born into, the families we create, the families we make through the people we choose as friends. This is where we create our lives, this is where we find meaning, and this is where our purpose becomes clear.

Family is where we first experience love and where we first give it. It's probably the first place where we've been hurt by someone we love, and if we're fortunate, it's the place where we learn that love can overcome even the most painful rejection. This crucible of love is where we start to ask those big spiritual questions, and ultimately it's where they end.

I have seen such expressions of love. A husband who gently washes his wife's face with a cool washcloth, cupping the back of her bald head in his hand to get to the nape of her neck because she is too weak to lift it from the pillow. A daughter spooning pudding into the mouth of her mother, a woman who has not recognized her for years. A wife arranging the pillow under the head of her husband's no-longer-breathing body before she helps the undertaker lift him onto the waiting stretcher.

The meaning of our lives cannot be found in books or lecture halls or even churches or synagogues. It's discovered through these acts of love. If God is love, and I believe that to be true, then we learn about God when we learn about love. The first, and usually the last, classroom of love is the family.

The remarkable thing about this crucible of love is that the love we experience in our families doesn't have to be perfect. In fact, it can't be perfect, because none of us is perfect.

Sometimes, that love is not only imperfect, it seems to be missing entirely. Monstrous things happen in families. Too often, more often than I want to believe possible, patients tell me what it feels like when the person they love beats them or rapes them. They tell me what it feels like to know that they're utterly unwanted by their parents. They tell me what it feels like to be the target of someone's rage. They tell me what it feels like to know that they abandoned their children, or that their drinking destroyed their family, or that they failed to care for those who needed them.

Even in these cases, I am amazed at the strength of the human soul. Even the people who did not know love in their families know that they *should* have been loved. They somehow know love by its absence. They somehow know what was missing, and what they deserved as children and adults.

When the love is imperfect, or a family is destructive, something else can be learned: forgiveness. The spiritual work of being human is learning how to love and how to forgive.

That work is the gift we give each other, for there is little in this world people long for more than to be loved and to be forgiven by their mothers and fathers, daughters and sons.

GLORIA'S BABY

Gloria picked up a strawberry from the bowl in front of her and handed it to me. She had two over-the-bed tables, the type you'd find in a hospital, on either side of her recliner. They were covered with catalogs and magazines, get-well cards from friends who no longer came to visit, cell phone and television remote, notepad and pen, lip balm and tissues, bottles of water, books of crossword puzzles, and a crocheting project I never once saw her pick up or make any progress on — all the things she might need at any time. She would swing one table in front and over her legs and the other out of the way with a practiced hand. Today, the table in front of her had a big bowl full of strawberries, and a much smaller bowl full of strawberry stems.

She was gleeful about those strawberries. She ate each one in a single huge bite, emptying one bowl and filling the other with remarkable speed.

"These make me feel like I'm a little girl again on the farm, out in the sunshine," she said. "You know, I can't remember the last time I spent a day out in the sunshine." Then, "Course, I don't miss the heat, being out in the fields, you understand. Just the sunshine. I miss that feeling."

"Did you grow up on a farm?" I asked.

"No, no," she said quickly. "I just spent a lot of time there when I was a child."

The conversation meandered somewhere else, but in a few minutes she grew quiet and pensive. She picked up another strawberry and ate it very slowly, with her eyes closed.

"I want to tell you a story," she said.

"Every Sunday after church, we all came home and put on our work clothes. My grandmother came to pick us up in her big car, and we, me and my brothers and my father, we all drove out to the country to a farm. It was the farm of a black family. Not a very big farm, and kind of falling apart because there was no farmer. He was dead. It was just his wife out there, trying to hold on.

"We'd go out there, and we would work our fingers to the bone, all of us. Even my grandmother. We were out in the fields, helping with harvesting and pulling weeds. Even when I was real little, I picked up stones out of the dirt so they could plow. We worked in the house and the barns, fixing whatever needed fixing, cleaning whatever needed cleaning.

"I didn't mind, though. I actually really liked it, because there were half a dozen children out there that we could play with. We went down to the creek and played hide-and-go-seek. We built forts and fairy lands, and played little jokes on each other. We had so much fun. Their mother would have a huge dinner waiting for us, and later there was supper, too. I loved going out there.

"But I never knew just who they were, or why we went there. We never visited with any other black folks. Just that family. We never went to any other farm. Just that one.

"I asked when I was little, but was always told to hush. I asked once, when I was a teenager, who they were and why we went out there every single Sunday, but my mother slapped me hard across the face and told me to never ask again. So I didn't.

"When I grew up and got married and had my own children, I stopped going out there. I don't know if my father and grandmother continued, because I never asked. It was just not something we could talk about. Ever.

"And then I sort of forgot. Not really, but I never thought about it after a while. We never talked about that family, and I never saw them again. I don't think I ever knew their last name.

"Years went by. And then, at my grandmother's funeral, a black woman walked up to me. She threw her arms around me. 'Do you recognize me?' she asked.

"Well, I was totally confused. 'No,' I said.

" 'I'm Betty,' she said. 'From the farm? On Sundays? We used to play together when we were little girls.' And then I did recognize her. I hadn't seen her since I was a teenager, but I knew her.

"And then. Well, my goodness. Then she said, 'I'm your cousin.'

"Kerry, I just stood there with my mouth open. That whole family — they were my cousins. My own flesh and blood. My father's brother had fallen in love with a black woman. They lived together in secret out in the country and had children. But then he died, leaving them alone out there, one woman and five little kids to run the farm.

"That's why we all went out there and worked till our fingertips bled. Because she couldn't do it alone. They were my cousins, my father's nieces and nephews, my grandmother's grandchildren."

Gloria sat back in her recliner and threw her hands out to the sides and laughed. "All along, they were my cousins."

"And you had no idea, all those years?"

"Nope. It was a big secret."

"But Betty knew?" I asked. "She knew at the funeral. Had she just found out, too?"

"Oh no, she knew all her life. They all knew all along, the black children. Even the little ones, they knew who we were and who they were."

"But wait!" I think I shook my head. "The children knew all along, when you came out to visit on Sundays, that you were cousins, and they never told you? Why not?"

"Because they were all sworn to secrecy not to tell anyone until my grandmother died."

"Why?"

"Because of her shame. They had to keep the secret of who they really were."

"Your grandmother's shame?" I asked.

"Of having black grandchildren."

"But she — all of you — went out there every Sunday. Of her entire life, until she died? Even though she was so ashamed?"

"Well, they were still her grandchildren,"

Gloria said, seemingly puzzled by my questions. "I know they kept it a secret because they were trying to protect me."

"Protect you how?" I asked.

"Kerry?" She started laughing again. "Do you really not understand? From knowing that I had black family. From knowing my uncle had run away with a Negro woman. I reckon that's why they kept it hid, to keep me protected."

"But protected from what?"

"Well, I guess from the shame. They didn't want me to have to carry the shame, too." She sighed, and I could tell it was time for me to be quiet. "Times were just different then. We had so many secrets in my family."

There are so many secrets out there in the world. I carry around some of them, secrets that have been entrusted to me by patients and family members. Most of them are personal secrets about the teller, secrets about things they did, things they thought or felt or wished, things they didn't think they could ever tell. Things that happened to them, things done to them when they were small, or helpless, or desperate. Secrets about the self.

But some of the secrets I've been privy to were elaborate, family-held secrets. Secrets with multiple participants and levels of understanding. Secrets held across generations that demanded that children be complicit in their own shame, like Gloria's cousins.

Because that's what secrets are about — shame.

Shame, along with the belief that keeping a secret will protect you or someone else, comes from the idea that there is some part of us so monstrous, so terrible, so inhuman, that it must not be known. The intense humiliation and pain of being shamed for a perceived transgression just reinforces the need to keep the secret. Shame-filled secrets are told — when they are told at all — with bodies trembling and voices shaking so hard they are barely comprehensible, with fear and urgency in equal measure, throbbing with the enormous energy it has taken to keep them secret for so long.

Why, after so many years, do people tell me their secrets? I don't think it's for forgiveness. I'm not a priest, rabbi, or pastor. I can't offer some sort of sacramental absolution or formal forgiveness on behalf of God. No, when someone shares a shameful secret with me, it doesn't feel like confession. It feels like an unburdening.

The great mid-century cultural anthropologist Ruth Benedict wrote about the differences between cultures based on shame and those based on guilt. Guilt and shame aren't the same thing. In fact, they're opposites.

In a guilt-based culture, society enforces its norms and rules by instilling an internal moral compass in people that tells them when they do something wrong. When they violate it, they feel bad about what they have done and how it affects others. The guilt is over the wrongdoing, and it's internally generated. Even if no one else ever knew about the transgression, it sparks guilt.

In a shame-based culture, on the other hand, social control comes from a sense of honor or duty, and a sense of wrongdoing comes from the fear of being shamed and ostracized by other people. Break a social norm and your honor is damaged — *you* are indelibly damaged — and the honor of your family as well. Shame comes from other people knowing. Shame is based on pain and fear; it works because the person being shamed experiences emotional and psychic pain and, as a result, fears ever being shamed again. Sometimes a person is cast out of her community, physically harmed, or even killed for doing something seen as shameful. Hence, the desire to keep shameful things secret.

While a culture may rely more heavily on either shame or guilt for social control, they're not mutually exclusive; people can feel both. Shame plays as great a role in people's spiritual lives as guilt does, because it poses an existential problem. When people feel shame, they believe that there is something intrinsically wrong with their very person, with their soul. Shame comes from who you believe you *are,* not just what you've done or felt.

I was deeply ashamed of having been psychotic. I thought the very core of me was obliterated, or utterly ruined at best.

That shame came from the enormous stigma around mental illness in our society. It might be acceptable to introduce the topic of postpartum depression into discussions with a group of other mothers, but bringing up postpartum psychosis was a sure path to becoming a pariah. As a sympathetic (and beloved) psychiatrist once said to me, "We just don't have support groups for people with drug-induced psychotic disorder caused by anesthesia during childbirth."

While good friends tried to reassure me that I just "wasn't myself" when I was psychotic, who exactly was I?

I had one answer for that: I was a bad

mother. That the birth had gone so spectacularly badly didn't seem to me to indicate medical complications and poor decisions on an anesthesiologist's part. It seemed to mean that I was, at my very core, a failure as a mother. I mean, really, whose first attempt at birth goes like that? I felt like I was cursed.

The corollary to all that shame: secrets. I learned, the hard way, not to tell people what had happened to me.

But the problem with secrets is that they are exhausting. And while they might protect what people see as their most vulnerable places, that protection comes at an enormous cost.

"I have another story to tell you," Gloria said, several weeks later. She had steadily gotten sicker and weaker, so that we were now visiting for the first time in her bedroom instead of the living room. Despite her exhaustion, though, she had insisted on getting up and dressed and in her chair.

We'd been having a good time talking about the indignity of Gloria having to accept help from her neighbor, Ronald, with bathing and bathroom. Many Southern women of her age might have been embarrassed, but Gloria found it hilarious that the last man who would probably see her naked was an unemployed forty-year-old gay man. "So it's come to this," she laughed.

Then she stopped laughing and bit her lips.

"And it's not just a story I want to tell you. You have to do something for me."

"I'll try. I'll always try," I said.

"You've got to do better than try." She turned away from me and stared straight ahead of her, silent. This was really unlike her. In a minute or so, she began to talk.

"I got pregnant when I was nineteen," she started. Unlike other times, she didn't laugh as she told this story, and she didn't really seem to be telling it to me. She spoke slowly, laboriously, and paused after each sentence with a look of slight shock on her face, as though surprised by what she'd just said. She seemed almost to be in a trance. But she didn't hesitate. She told it as if compelled, as if once she'd begun, nothing could make her stop.

"I wasn't married. It was my best friend's boyfriend. They had broken up. He asked me to go for a drive. I'd never had a boyfriend, and I was flattered.

"I'd never had sex before, and I didn't know what was happening. It was . . . it was confusion. I was foolish. So foolish.

"Later, by the time I figured out I was pregnant, he and my best friend had gotten back together and gotten engaged. She was so happy. I couldn't tell her.

"Now, I wasn't a girl. I was a full-grown woman, with a job as a secretary. But I still lived at my parents' house and I never knew anything about sex. That seems crazy, I know, but I didn't. When I told my parents, my father . . . oh my God, my father.

"He was so strict. He was the strictest father in the world. We weren't even allowed to wear skirts above the knee or a smudge of lipstick. I wasn't allowed to pluck my eyebrows. And then to get pregnant. To get pregnant. Oh my Lord. I thought he would kill me.

"But instead they sent me away. He and my mother both. She agreed to it, my mother. They said it was the only way. I had to go, because I had nowhere else to live. No one to marry, not enough money to raise a baby, and once anyone figured out I was pregnant, I'd lose my job anyway. So what choice did I have? What choice did I have? No choice. I had no choice.

"Things were different back then, so different. I was trapped. Women like me, we ended up garbage. I didn't want to be garbage. I didn't want that. So I had to go.

"The home was in Charleston. I'd never been to Charleston before, but we weren't allowed to go out and explore. We just stayed in, me and the other girls there. Six months later, I had my baby.

"Some of the people there said I shouldn't look at him, because it would make it harder to give him up. Because that's what I was going to do. That's what I had to do.

"I came back to my mother's and father's house a few days later. When they picked me up, they didn't ask about it. I didn't get the addresses of any of the other girls there. It was like it never even happened. I gave him up and had never even seen him.

"But the next day I knew I had made a mistake. I woke up and I couldn't breathe. With every drop of my soul, I knew I'd made a mistake. I was like a caged animal. I couldn't stop moving. I had made a terrible mistake. I had to get my baby back.

"I called up the home. I talked to the social worker. She was a Jewish woman from New York. Her name was Ruth. She was so skinny you couldn't believe she could stand up straight. But she was the most intimidating woman I'd ever met.

"Ruth said I couldn't have the baby back. I told her I had to have him back. She told me it was better for the baby to go to a family. I said I had to get him back. She said he would be better off without me, on account I had no money and no husband. I just kept telling her I had to get my baby back.

"Finally she said that if I wanted my baby back, I had to pay for him. I had to buy him back. I had to pay back all the money they'd spent on me. I had to pay for six months of room and board, and for the doctor visits, and for delivering the baby in the hospital, and for the baby's doctor visits and the formula they were giving him, and for the nurses who had taken care of him since he'd been born. She was sorry, but that was the rules.

"If I can do that, I asked, iffen I can do that, pay that money back, I can have him? I can have my baby?

"Yes, she said. But you'd be making a mistake, she said, in the calmest, angriest voice I ever heard. A terrible mistake, and it would be the worst thing for that baby and for you. You have no husband, no home of your own, not enough money to buy him shoes and clothes and food.

"I sold everything I had to raise that money. I sold my car. I sold my record player and all my records. I sold all my clothes except for one dress and one pair of shoes. I sold every gift anyone had ever given me, every bit of jewelry. I even sold my hair curlers. I used every penny of my savings. Finally I had enough money.

"When I told my parents I was going to get my baby, I thought my father would have a stroke, right there in the living room. I've never seen someone so angry. I was so scared. I thought I might turn to dust from the fear. But I knew I had to do this.

"They kicked me out. I went to my friends but they couldn't help me. I even told my best friend and her husband, my son's father. I don't know if he knew he was the daddy. But he looked right at me and said no. No, he would not help. I had nowhere to live.

"So finally, I went to my grandmother. She had a big farm out in the country. I told her what happened. I was afraid she would turn me out, too. But instead, she said, I will help you. You and your baby can live here, with me.

"She drove me to Charleston in her car. When we got there, Ruth, the Jewish social worker from New York, met us in her office. She asked me if I really wanted to do this. I just pushed the envelope of money onto the table. She looked at me real hard. She was never one to smile. And she didn't smile now. But her face was not so stiff, I thought.

Softer, maybe, I thought. I hoped.

"Ruth called a nurse to bring the baby in. He was a month old already. It was the first time I'd ever seen him.

"When the nurse brought him in, my grandmother stood up and walked over and reached out for him. But then Ruth stood up and got in between my grandmother and the baby. 'No,' she said. 'That's not how this is going to be.' She took the baby in her arms. I thought she was going to take the baby back, right in front of my eyes, take him away from me. I started to cry.

"But instead, she walked over to me where I was sitting stuck in the chair like a statue. She put him in my arms.

" 'She is his mother,' Ruth said to my grandmother. 'She gets to hold him.'

"Ruth turned to me then. 'I have never met a woman who was more a mother than you,' she said to me. 'You are his mother. Don't let anyone take him away from you. If you love him like this all his life, he will be fine.' She still didn't smile, but she put her hands on my arms and squeezed, harder than I ever would have thought someone so skinny could squeeze.

"I have made so many mistakes in my life. This is the one thing I know I did right. It's the best thing I ever did in my whole life. I fought to get my baby back. I gave up everything to get my baby back. It's the greatest thing I ever did, or ever will do. I got my baby back."

Gloria stopped, out of breath from the exertion of telling me. She snapped out of her trance, and I did, too. She turned to look at me. Her face looked different. She pinned me with her eyes, drained but fierce.

"I want you to tell him," she said. "I'll give you his phone number and you will call up my son and tell him. I want him to know. His father was always so mean to him, and I want my boy to understand that it wasn't him. His father was mean because he resented him. My son wasn't his baby. I married him when my son was a year old, but he never came to love him right. I thought he would, I told myself he would, but he never did. I want my son to know it wasn't because there was something deep wrong about him. I think he always thought that. He knew his father didn't love him right. I want my baby to know why before I die. Will you call him and tell him his father wasn't his real father? Pull out your phone and I'll give you his number, and you call when you leave here."

I stumbled and stammered. I'm not sure

why I was so shocked by her request. Maybe it's because I usually only listen. I don't act. I was unprepared, and unsure how to tell Gloria I couldn't do what she was asking.

She stared at me as I sat there with my mouth hanging open. Finally she said, "It's just a phone call."

I pulled myself together and said, as gently as I could, "I think that's something you need to tell him."

Gloria had been calm the whole time she told me the story, but now tears welled in her eyes and her hands began to shake.

"I can't tell him. I just can't. Please. You have to tell him."

"I think that might be a bit of a shock, Gloria, if I called him out of the blue and told him that his father isn't really his father. He doesn't even know me."

"He would be relieved. He would be happy. There's no other way." She began to cry.

"You could tell him," I said as gently as I could.

"No! No I can't!"

"Why not?"

"Because —" And here she could barely speak. She shook so hard that the recliner shook underneath her. "Because what —" She sounded like she might choke. "Because what if" — she was almost hyperventilating — "what if he doesn't think it was a good thing that I went back for him?"

The thought hung heavy in the air.

I've learned over the years that these heavy, painful, anguish-filled moments — and believe me, they are anguish-filled for me, too — these moments when I so badly want to say something to break the tension, are exactly the moments I need to stay silent. They are the moments I need to hold still, and hold that sacred space open. Because when I can hold still and hold on in that place, no matter how hard it is for both of us, something can happen.

Gloria shook and cried for a little while, but for far less time than you might think. Now that she had given voice to her greatest fear, she could examine it.

"What if he doesn't think the best thing I ever did was a good thing at all? What if the social worker was right? What if he wishes I had left him at that unwed mothers home? What if he wishes some other family had adopted him? That he had a different mother? What if he wishes I had never gone back for him?"

I listened, and I waited. I knew I didn't have the answers, but I'd also been at this sort of juncture often enough to know that the patient does, somewhere deep inside. Maybe not the answers to the questions they've just asked, but the answers to the deeper questions that lie under the fear.

Gloria closed her eyes. For a moment I thought she might be so worn out that she had fallen asleep, but then she continued.

"It's amazing that you can love someone so much when you have never even met him. I loved my son so much and I didn't even know him. How is that possible? How is it possible to love someone so much that you're willing to give up your whole life, but you don't even know him?

"I want him to know, because I want him to know how much I love him. That I loved him before I even knew him. That I love him not because of who he is, but just because he is. That's what I want him to know."

What if the thing you consider to be your greatest accomplishment is not seen that way by anyone else? What if the thing you are proudest of is also the thing you are most ashamed of? What if your great love is also your deepest secret?

People keep secrets in a desperate and often ultimately futile attempt to protect themselves or the people they love. They think that the secret will be a bulwark against rejection and public humiliation, and so they carry it, no matter the weight. In so many cases, people keep secrets and even lie to each other out of love, and not malice.

What they may not realize is that in holding on so fiercely to what they see as shameful secrets, they're actually strengthening that system of shame. Keeping a secret is like fertilizing a weed, and the family secrets that fertilize shame choke out love before it can even grow. The secrets themselves, instead of protecting anyone from shame, become a source of it instead. Shame is the enemy of love; it can never serve it.

I don't know what it was like for Gloria's cousin Betty to have to carry the secret of her identity since she was a small child, to know that her grandmother saw her as a source of shame. I never got to meet Betty. But I can imagine, and what I imagine makes me want to cry.

Did Betty's cruel burden protect Gloria from pain? Of course not. The only thing that secret protected either woman from was each other's love and support. Gloria commented more than once at the sadness of missing out on decades of Betty's life.

Yet, even knowing this, Gloria kept the

secret of her son's birth from him. She wanted to protect him from what she felt was her shame and, by extension, his shame. It simply kept her from sharing the enormity of her love. Now, even as she lay dying, desperate for him to know, she still was not sure she could break through that shame and explain the depth of her love. Fear of rejection and humiliation still held its grip, after a lifetime in a stew of secrets.

What if the person you love the most does not love you back? What happens if you pour your love into the world and are rejected? Do you pour your love out anyway? Is it worth the risk? Is love stronger than shame?

These were Gloria's real questions.

Every visit thereafter, Gloria asked me to call her son. She pleaded, she begged. She was desperate for her son to know, and convinced she could not do it herself. At first, trying to talk about why she was too afraid to tell him herself just caused her more anguish, so I sidestepped her requests as gracefully as I could. I asked her to tell me the story again and again, to get it right when it was time to tell him.

Within a few weeks, Gloria had a new suggestion. "You tell him and I could sit next to you."

"That might could work," I said.

She told me again what she wanted me to say.

A few weeks later she said, "I might could tell him and you could sit next to me."

"That might could work," I said.

Then she practiced what she would say to him with me.

The week after that, she said, "I told my son when he was here the weekend."

"How did it go?"

She smiled and began to cry. But then she began to laugh as she cried, as she always did, and she couldn't speak.

If I Had Only Known, I Would Have Danced More

"I know I'm supposed to hate my body," Cynthia said in her soothing, liquid Southern drawl. She pushed away her lunch, a brown lump and pile of orange. Her daughter spent a lot of money to have low-fat, no-sodium, no-sugar, low-calorie meals prepared and delivered to the house while she was at work and Cynthia was home alone. They looked like piles of wet rocks.

"I really could die happy if I was allowed just one more bite of caramel cake," she said with a sigh. "I don't suppose you have any?"

"No, sorry. But why are you supposed to hate your body?"

"Well, Kerry!" She looked incredulous that I even asked. Then she laughed. "Because I'm fat!"

Cynthia ran her soft hands over her ponderous breasts and her mounding, cancer-ridden belly. She spilled over the sides of her recliner. "I've known that since I was little." She examined the crocheted blanket on her lap.

"Everyone told me — my family, my school, my church. When I got older, magazines and salesgirls and boyfriends — even if they didn't say so out loud. The world's been telling me for seventy-five years that my body is bad. First for being female, then for being fat, and then for being sick. I know they think it's terrible." She looked up, and this time tears trembled along her bottom eyelids. "But the one thing I never did understand is, why does everyone else want me to hate my body? What does it matter to them?"

There are many regrets and many unfulfilled wishes that patients have shared with me in the months or weeks before they die. But the time wasted spent hating their bodies, ashamed, abusing it or letting it be abused — the years, decades, or, in some cases, whole lives that people spent not appreciating their body until they were so close to leaving it — are some of the saddest.

Because unlike the foolish or best-intentioned mistakes, the terrible accidents, the slipups that irrevocably changed a life — unlike all those kinds of regrets — this one is not a tragic mistake. It's intentional.

It's something other people teach us to feel about our bodies. It's something other people want us to believe.

Sometimes it's media and peer pressure that create this shame, shame based on how we look. We're made ashamed of our weight or our body hair, our crooked teeth or our droopy eyes.

Sometimes it comes from the pastor and Sunday school teacher and lessons at home that begin at birth and seep in along with mother's milk, lessons about the sinfulness of the body. Some women grow up thinking that their very existence in a body that might be sexually attractive to someone else is cause for shame — that their bodies make bad things happen just by being.

Either way, the result of the messages is the same: lives lived thinking that bodies are something to criticize, to despise, or at best something to tolerate. A problem that cannot be corrected.

Too often, it's only as people realize that they will lose their bodies that they finally appreciate how truly wonderful the body is.

"I am going to miss this body so much," a different patient, many decades younger, said. She held up her hands in the dim light that seeped through the sunshade on the window. She stared at them as though she had never seen them before. "I'd never admit it to my husband and kids, but it's my own body I'll miss most of all. This body that danced and ate and swam and had sex and made babies. It's amazing to think about it. This body actually made my children. It carried me through this world."

She put her hands down. "And I'm going to have to leave it. I don't have a choice. And to think I spent all those years criticizing how it looked, and never noticing how good it felt. Until now when it never feels good."

Second in intensity to the regret of hating their bodies is the wish of the dying that they had appreciated their bodies in the course of their lives.

Mind you, it isn't just health that they wish they had appreciated. It is embodiment itself. It's the very experience of being in a body, something you might take for granted until faced with the reality that you won't have a body soon. No matter what you believe happens after death, whether it be an afterlife, reincarnation, or nothing at all, this remains: You will no longer be able to experience this world in this body, ever again. People who are dying face that reality every day.

So they talk about their favorite memories

of their bodies. About how the apples they stole from the orchard on the way home from school tasted, and how their legs and lungs burned as they ran away. The feel of the water the first time they went skinny-dipping. The smell of their babies' heads. The breeze on their skin that time they made love outside.

And dancing. So many stories about dancing. I can't count the hundreds of times people — more men than women — have closed their eyes and said, when describing USO dances during World War II, or shagging at South Carolina beach houses, or long, exuberant nights dancing at road-houses and discos and barns and wherever else there were bodies and music, "If I had only known, I would have danced more."

If you accept the idea that each of us should love our neighbors as we love ourselves, what does it mean that so many voices out there insist that your body, my body, every-one's body is something to despise because it is too fat, too ugly, too sexual, too old, or too brown? That we teach one another, in thousands of blatant and quiet ways, to think we are shameful? That the body is something to be overcome, or beaten into submission, or despised? If I am supposed to hate my body, am I supposed to hate yours, too? I look around, and it certainly seems that way. How do these voices telling us that we are supposed to hate our bodies affect our notions of how we should care for the sick, the disabled, the elderly, the young? For mothers, soldiers, workers, immigrants, men, women? What we believe about our bodies affects how we treat other bodies, and how we treat one another's bodies is how we treat one another.

"You know what, Kerry?" Cynthia asked as she ran the sleeve of her nightgown across her eyes. "Even though I'm fat, even though I've had this cancer for twenty years, and I haven't had any hair in I can't remember how long — even though all that, I don't hate my body. They were wrong, and they always have been. I think because I thought I was going to die for so long, I figured it out. And that's why I've been happy anyway. I just need to figure out how to get some caramel cake into the house."

WHERE THERE'S BREATH, THERE'S HOPE

"We can go outside and smoke a cigarette together, if you want," Reggie said. "You just gotta wheel me down."

"I don't smoke, but I'll go with you. It'll be nice to sit outside," I said.

"Nah. Forget it. It's no fun to smoke alone."

Reggie had chronic obstructive pulmonary disease. Basically, he was slowly suffocating to death. Each day, he was a little less able to take a deep breath. Each day, a little less able to get oxygen, a little more winded. People with COPD are aware at all times of how they'll die. They'll die struggling for a breath, and they know what that will feel like because they're doing it all day, every day, right now. Except it will be worse, much worse.

Not surprisingly, people with COPD are what hospice workers sometimes call "needy." They need a lot of attention. If you're really, really frustrated with the Reggies of the world, you call them "attention seekers."

Of course, when we call someone needy, it really means that we don't have the time, the energy, the inclination, or the capacity to meet their need. We blame the need, or worse, the person with the need, instead of the lack of time, energy, inclination, or capacity. It's not easy for heath care workers to admit we aren't meeting a need. After all, most people went into this work to try to help people. We're trained to recognize, assess, and meet needs. That's what we do. So when our efforts are falling short, when we are simply not enough, when we're suffocating in a patient's neediness, it feels terrible. It's easier to blame the patient than to acknowledge how very limited any one of us is in the face of a disease like COPD.

Reggie lived in the public nursing home, an enormous and grand-from-the-outside building that had been built as a maternity hospital almost a hundred years ago. The inside was significantly less grand, but the nurses and aides worked hard, with little in the way of amenities. Murals of the outdoors were painted in the hallways. Leaded casement windows in the rooms let in sunlight and sometimes made rainbows on the walls. But it was a nursing home. An institution is an institution, no matter how loving the staff or regal the building.

Reggie pulled a white plastic cart on wheels over to the bedside. His short legs dangled over the side of the mattress and didn't touch the floor.

"Well, hang on. Lemme see what I got in here. I know I got something." He rummaged through the clear plastic drawers full of random stuff — rubber gloves, packs of gum, paperbacks, tissues, tubes of lip balm, magazines.

"Hah!" he said triumphantly. He pulled out four cellophane packets of mostly uncrushed saltines and a tiny tub of strawberry jelly with gold foil on top. "Would you like some?" he asked almost shyly, as he extended two packets of wrapped crackers to me.

"Thanks, Reggie."

"I wish I had something to drink to give you."

"The crackers are perfect."

"What's your name again?"

"Kerry."

"Oh, that's right. So, Kerry, I've been thinking about my lung transplant again."

"Oh yeah?"

As a chaplain, I don't decide what a patient and I will talk about. I listen to what's on the patient's mind, what's burdening him or giving him great joy that particular day. Reggie wanted to talk about a lung transplant. All the time.

When I first started visiting, he wanted to talk logistics. Where his transplant would take place, what he needed to get in place for it to happen, the letters he had written to various doctors and transplant centers. What might have happened (or was going to happen) to the poor soul who was going to donate his lungs to Reggie. His hopes for what his life would be like once he got the transplant. He would move out of the nursing home and find his own apartment, maybe on the water. He'd buy a boat, a little Boston Whaler, and go fishing. He might even reconnect with his sister, whom he had not seen in thirty years. Maybe he would even look up his ex-wife, whom he'd left decades ago. Talking about a lung transplant made him happy. I listened.

Over time, though, talking about the lung transplant started to make him angry. He was angry at the nursing home nurses, who either ignored his transplant plan or thought it was cute. I can understand that anger: Imagine that there's only one thing that you think can save you, and you've hung your hope on it, and the people you rely on for your very survival think your hope for survival is just darling.

But Reggie's real rage and frustration were reserved for Stacy, the hospice nurse, and Sue, the social worker. These were the two people, in his mind, who had the power to save him. Every time they visited, he peppered them with demands, wanting to know why they were not getting everything in place for the transplant. They had power and clout and connections. He had none of those things. No one would take him seriously. He vented his rage and frustration and impotence.

Here's the thing about Reggie's lung transplant: It was never going to happen. Ever. He would not survive surgery. Stacy had explained to him dozens of times that he physically did not qualify for a transplant. Sue had explained it again and again, as well. They grew frustrated with him, with his passive-aggressive manipulations, his temper, the nasty things he said, his unwillingness to accept reality. There were dozens of other patients to see, and Reggie was needy and demanding. He needed to talk about that transplant, he demanded that they do something, and he would not or could not accept what they told him. Reggie believed that the nurse and social worker had the power to grant his wish, and they were not using it. He believed that they could make it happen, if they wanted to. So he hounded them.

Me, the chaplain, I had no power. A chaplain brings nothing. Unlike the nurse, I have no medication to give; unlike the social worker, I have no programs to sign up for. I don't take anything, either — no urine samples, no vital signs, no signatures on documents. I don't make anything happen.

All I can do is show up and listen. This, as strange as it sounds, is where a chaplain's power lies, in the powerlessness of the role. Because there was no point in hounding me to get the transplant going, Reggie didn't. We could just be there together. He could stop fighting, even if it was just for that hour. He didn't have to demand anything, and I didn't have to become a "bad guy" in his mind.

When Reggie vented his frustration to me, his fury would eventually burn out. Then he'd grow wistful. He would imagine. He would imagine a different life for himself.

"Wouldn't it be great if I could take a deep breath?"

"Yeah, it'd be wonderful."

"Wouldn't it be great if I could get outta here?"

"Yeah, I really wish you could, Reg."

"I'd get a little dog. Just a mutt."

"What would you name him?"

"Don't know," he said. "I could even come and visit you and your family. You got kids?"

"I do."

"I could take 'em fishing."

"Wouldn't that be something?"

"New lungs is the only way any of that could happen."

"A lung transplant would let you do all that, and get out of here."

"See, you understand how important this is. You understand what I want."

"You want a lung transplant because you want to live, and that's a reasonable thing to want."

"Yeah. Exactly. It's reasonable. It's not crazy. I want another chance to live. I want to start over again. I want to live a good life."

Because Reggie had not lived a good life. It wasn't just that bad things had happened to him. No, it's that he did bad things to other people. For a living.

Talking about the lung transplant became a way of talking about life, and about the life he'd led, and the life he wished he had led instead. Reggie had literally no one at the end of his life — not a single friend, lover, or family member. Just half-coherent memories of the violence he had committed on a regular basis his entire life.

I couldn't give Reggie new lungs, but I could offer him the most powerful thing a chaplain, or any of us, has: my presence. Reggie and I could talk about hope for something new and regret for what had been. Because that's what he was really talking about. The lung transplant was really a way to talk about hope and hope's flip side, regret. In quiet moments, not at every visit but more than once, Reggie would bow his head all the way down, swing his legs back and forth under the edge of the bed, and say, "I'm not stupid. It ain't gonna happen. But I can't let it go."

Deep down, Reggie knew that he couldn't have that transplant. But giving up on the quest would be to give up on hope, and that was something he just couldn't do.

Now he had less than six months left to live. Those six months would be spent in a tiny room with a leaded glass window on the sixth floor of a municipal nursing home that had once been a maternity hospital, with a plastic cart full of tiny salt and pepper packets and books of already-completed crossword puzzles, alone with his thoughts.

The lung transplant was a vehicle — like that little Boston Whaler. It was a vehicle to his long-lost sister, his long-left wife, my children, whom he'd never met, and to me, whose name he could never remember. It was a way to other human beings, with whom he'd connected so little.

Reggie wanted to talk about the lung transplant because that was his hope. His great hope not just for survival, but for a chance to redo his life. To live again, but this time differently.

If not a lung transplant, what could his hope be?

When my father died, I decided that I'd live my life in such a way that I would never again have any regrets. I even wrote that down as a promise to myself on a piece of paper.

That I thought such a thing was feasible just shows how young I was when he died.

I've never met a single patient who didn't have at least some regrets. Not all of these regrets were as deep as Reggie's. Most people haven't done such regrettable things.

But there is always something to regret, even in a joy-filled life. A woman — mother of five and happily married for forty years — regrets dropping out of college to marry her sweetheart. A farmer who never moved away from the town where he'd grown up wonders what would have happened if he had stayed in Japan after the war for even a year or two, as his commanding officer asked, instead of rushing home to the family pecan orchard that gave him such contentment in his life.

Life is a million choices, and every choice is a choice not to do something else, and so regrets accrue with life. It's inevitable. Thinking through those regrets, though, gives any one of us a chance to think about what we wish had been different. It's a chance to think about what we feel is missing in our lives, what we hope could be different. Most important, even if just in a small way, it's a chance to act on that understanding.

Hope is the belief that better things are possible. Regret shows us what those better things we hope for are. Regret hones hope, sharpens and clarifies the desire at the heart of it. If you're alive, even if you're on hospice, you can still work on making those hopes come true.

As a very young woman, I thought regret was a failure, something to avoid at all costs.

It is, in fact, a window. It's an unasked-for chance, an uncomfortable prompt, a painful encouragement to imagine what else could be. If you let it, regret can be a vehicle to hope. But you have to accept it first. You have to hold it up to the light streaming in from those leaded casement windows, in order to see clearly what it is that you wish was different in your life.

There may be thousands of regrets in a single life. Hope, though, can take millions of forms. Hope is a shape-shifter that can appear and grow in even the tiniest of cracks, at even the last hour. People sometimes ask what hope could mean for a hospice patient who has no hope for a cure, no hope for returning to the life they had once known and loved. What could hope possibly look like to someone who is dying? It can mean anything. It could look like everything.

Reggie's regret was how empty and alone his life was. His hope was for connection, perhaps even love. He yearned for that. He didn't have much to work with. His ex-wife wasn't coming back. Neither was his sister. He had pushed away every aide and nurse with his demands. His very neediness seemed to ensure that his need for love at

79

the end of his life would never be met, that his hope for connecting with another person, finally, would come to nothing.

It was Patrick who was on call the night Reggie died. Reggie had requested the chaplain, and when Patrick arrived, Reggie looked at him and asked where the girl with the blue eyes was. When Patrick explained that he was the chaplain for the night, Reggie turned and faced the wall.

Was that me? Patrick asked the next day, and did I know the patient? Yes, I said, that was me. Of course I knew him.

Here's the surprising thing: At that time, I had not seen Reggie for almost six months. I was no longer assigned to his nursing home. We had said good-bye a long time ago, and even then, he didn't know my name, had seemed unconcerned that he would be meeting with a new chaplain instead of me. I wasn't sure I had made any sort of connection with Reggie at all. But maybe, just maybe, our being present with each other had been enough. Maybe in those meetings over saltines and strawberry jelly, his hope for connection had in some small way been met. I hope so.

LIVING IN THE GRAY

"I set a trap," Frank said when a commercial came on during *The Price Is Right*.

The Price Is Right was Frank's favorite show, and after I said some prayers with his wife, Alice, we always watched together for a while and talked.

"What do you mean?" I asked.

"To figure out who was stealing the medicine. I set a trap and I figured out who it is."

For the past two months, the hospice team had been up in arms about missing painkillers. At first, the pill count of OxyContin was coming up short at every nurse's visit. Peggy, the nurse case manager, and Christy, the hospice team manager, wondered if Frank was having trouble remembering or seeing how many pills he had already crushed into Alice's pudding when he was preparing her lunch. She'd been bedridden for the past ten years with a painful neurodegenerative disease, and now Frank himself was quite elderly.

Peggy had switched Alice over to liquid morphine, hoping it would be easier for Frank to administer. But then the morphine, too, started coming up short.

Peggy thought Frank might be spilling the medicine, or pouring the wrong amount. She decided to pre-fill syringes for him, so that there was no chance of his measuring out the wrong dosage, or of his arthritic hands tipping the small bottle. He could just squirt the right amount in Alice's mouth.

But the next week, some of the filled syringes were missing.

In hospice, this is a big deal. Medicines like morphine are a key piece in battling shattering pain and allowing patients and families to enjoy their time together. They can seem like miracles for people with excruciating and chronic pain. But these are also narcotics, Schedule II drugs that are highly regulated because they're abused by addicts.

Now it was no longer a question of whether Frank was mishandling the drug. Someone was stealing it.

Suspicion fell on everyone who could possibly have access to the kitchen refrigerator where it was stored — meaning everyone who came into the apartment: the hospice workers, the private aides the family hired, Frank and Alice's children and their spouses, and the grandchildren.

This idea — that the culprit could have been a family member — was just about too much for Frank to bear. So he set out to discover for himself who was stealing the morphine, with an elaborate plan involving locks and timers.

He was so happy when he told me that he had figured out who it was. It was Jessica, one of the private aides.

"You're sure of it?" I asked.

"Yes! I just told you how I know for certain."

"Have you told Peggy yet?"

"Why would I tell Peggy?" he said. "I'm not telling anyone. I just wanted to make sure it wasn't someone in my own family."

"Frank, I need to tell my boss."

"What do you mean? You can't tell her. You promised me. I made you promise."

Dread washed over me, because this was true. I had made a promise. As soon as I walked in, Frank had asked me if I could keep a secret. "Of course," I'd answered.

"You promise?" he'd asked.

"Yes," I'd said. "I promise."

It was a stupid answer, if I'm being honest. An imprecise answer, if I'm trying to make myself feel better about it. Because while I certainly can keep many secrets, there are some things that, as a chaplain and a hospice team member, I have to report. Elder abuse is one of them. And someone stealing desperately needed and federally controlled pain medication from a sick and dying woman who needs it to make her life bearable counted as abuse. Also, it was illegal. Also, it put our work as a hospice at great risk. Also, making unprescribed morphine available to addicts put them in danger.

I had to tell, for so many reasons.

Except for the fact that I had promised not to.

"You're a chaplain. That's like a priest. If I tell you something in confession, you can't tell anyone."

"But I'm not a priest, Frank, and it wasn't confession."

"I told you things I never told nobody."

"I'd never share those things. But this is different. She's stealing from your wife, Frank. She's hurting your wife. Your wife whom you love so much."

"No she isn't. Peggy will just give me more morphine. If you tell, she'll go to jail.

84

Her kids will have no mother. Isn't that right?"

"I don't know what will happen to her," I admitted.

"I never would have told you if I'd known you didn't care about other people."

"Frank, I do care."

He stared straight ahead, past the tiny television in the corner of the room and out the small, high-set windows that let just a faint stream of light into the damp apartment. Alice's hospital bed took up most of the living room. We sat in two armchairs next to each other, facing her bed.

Finally, he turned to face me again. "You wanna tell a story? You know what you can tell them? You tell them this story. Everyone needs to know this story, 'cause this story is the real truth.

"There once was a kid I knew in our neighborhood, growing up. Eight years old. He saw his father beaten to death by four cops, right in front of him. When they were done, he ran over to his father and saw his brains spilling out of his head onto the street. Nothing ever happened to those cops. Not a thing.

"After that, his mother had to support his little brothers and sisters. She took in sewing and laundry and broke her back, but there was never enough to eat. He got so angry. He grew up into the angriest kid you ever met in your life.

"Then one day when he was fourteen years old, he saw one of the cops who'd killed his father in front of his eyes, and he killed him. With a knife. He stabbed him until he killed him.

"If you were to hear about some teenager who killed a cop, you would think he was a horrible person. You would say, Throw him in jail forever. But that's because you didn't know the whole story. You didn't know what had happened to him. You didn't know what he saw. You didn't know. And you don't know what you don't know. Instead you just judge.

"That guy grew up to be a good man who took care of his family. He started on the scallop boats and broke his back and worked his way up to first mate. He wasn't a bad person. You see what I'm saying now?

"It wasn't so black and white as it might seem to somebody from the outside. It was gray.

"It's the same with Jessica. I know her. She knows my wife. Jessica's Alice's favorite. She's gentle and patient with her. She's never rough. She's got little kids and nobody to help her. Nobody. Do you know how much money she gets paid by that agency? Eight dollars an hour. To raise those kids by herself.

"If she's selling that medicine so she can buy shoes for her kids, I'm okay with that. I can get more medicine for Alice. I know what it's like to be a kid with no shoes and then you can't go to school.

"That's why I'm not reporting her, and that's why you can't report her."

He paused for a few seconds to catch his breath. He was crying. "The world is not black and white. There is no black and white. There's only gray. You have to live in the gray, or you got no kindness in your heart. You gotta see the gray. You tell them that. You tell everyone that."

I walked out to my car and sat in the driver's seat for a very long time. I knew the aide, too, having met her a few times when our appointments overlapped. She always showed me and Frank pictures of her babies on her phone. Once she asked me to help her because she just didn't have enough strength in her arms, after working double shifts seven days in a row, to turn Alice with as much gentleness as she would like. She asked me at Christmastime if I wanted to buy some food stamps at a discount so she could have money for toys to give to her children, who were still young enough to believe in Santa Claus. I stammered and blushed, confused at what she was offering. I declined, not because it was illegal, but because I didn't know how to use food stamps. My life may have been hard when my children were babies, but hers was precarious and vulnerable in a way that mine never was.

Finally I called Grace, a fellow chaplain. Perhaps the greatest benefit of being a hospice chaplain is that you get to work with other hospice chaplains. Grace was much older, much more experienced, much wiser, and in general just a much better chaplain than I was. Grace was my chaplain, just as I was my patients' chaplain.

I told her the whole situation and asked her what I should do.

"Christy needs to know this," she said in her quiet, gravelly voice.

"I know. I know. I just feel horrible telling her, because he asked me not to."

"But there are other things at play here, other things besides his wishes. You need to act in the best interest of the patient. You need to follow the law. You need to think about our agency and the other patients who need us, who would be impacted if we were shut down. You need to think about the addicts who are being sold this medication."

"I know. I just can't get his voice and his face out of my head. I can't get his story out of my mind —"

Grace cut me off. "It's done. I already told her."

"What?"

"Well, I never promised not to tell Christy and Peggy. You did, but I didn't. So I sent an e-mail while we were talking. It's done."

Before I could say anything, my phone beeped. Another call — from Christy, my boss.

"I have to go," I said to Grace.

"Good luck."

Christy was not happy. "Were you really not going to tell me, Kerry?"

"No, of course I was. I just needed to sort it out in my head."

"What was there to sort? It's pretty clear-cut, Ker. There should have been nothing to sort out. It's black and white here."

But to Frank, and to me, it wasn't.

"You have to live in the gray, or you got no kindness in your heart," Frank had said. What did he mean by "the gray"? And what did that have to do with kindness?

I can't answer for Frank, but I can say why his words made me sit in the car for an hour.

When I was diagnosed with postpartum psychosis, I was put on a medication called Zyprexa. While it saved my life, it also made life difficult to live. I was better off than when I was suffering from bouts of catatonia that left me unable to move for hours at a time, but now I slept sixteen hours a day and gained sixty pounds in three months. I developed shooting pains up my legs and uncontrollable twitching in my feet. Walking felt like wading through waist-high wet concrete. My head felt like it was full of wet concrete, too, and even the most basic thought emerged only after intense concentration and struggle. I lived my days through to-do lists that reminded me to "brush teeth," "wash face," "get dressed," "change baby diaper." Any movement was exhausting, physically and mentally.

So though I was better, going shopping with a nine-month-old baby by myself was still beyond my capabilities. I needed new shoes that might help the pain in my feet, though, so my mother took me to Macy's, as if I were her little girl again.

While I tried on ugly shoes, slowly, slowly, slowly trying to get my muscles to move the way I needed them to, and attempted to force my brain to focus enough to make a choice about which shoes to buy — a task that seemed so difficult I didn't really understand how it could be done, by anyone, ever — my baby in his stroller grew frustrated. He began to squawk and twist around. While my mom went in search of a saleswoman to get a few different sizes for me to try, he began to cry.

I sat there, one shoe on and one shoe off, confused, exhausted, and feeling utterly defeated by what my life had become — at what I had become — and watched him cry while I waited for my mother to return and tell me what to do.

A woman sitting not too far away began to comment on the situation to her friend, loudly enough that I could hear her.

"What kind of mother just sits there and lets her baby cry?" she said. "Have you ever seen anything like this?" I sat and listened to her go on about me and my child. A crying baby, she noted, ought to be more important than a new pair of shoes. But apparently some people were just that selfish. Or was it lazy? If she had a baby, she would never let him cry like that. Why did women like that get to have a baby? A baby of hers would never cry like that.

My mom returned with a bigger pair of

shoes to fit my swollen feet. "Just hurry up and try them on," she encouraged as she turned to calm my baby.

But something in me snapped. That woman couldn't have known how sick I was, nor could she know how physically disabling the medication I was on was. She only judged by what she could see. What she saw seemed black and white to her. She gave me no benefit of the doubt, exercised no empathy to wonder what in the world was going on with me, my mother, and my son. I wanted her to understand that I was sick, and that I was doing the best I could. I wanted her to stop shaming me. I wanted her to understand that I was already so ashamed of what had happened and what I had become that I could barely cope. I wanted her to see that I was gray. I stood up — slowly — and walked over to her, one step in front of the other, as quickly as I could through the concrete. She and her friend looked at me with disgust. I didn't say any of the things I wanted to. I had no language for any of that then. Instead, I said: "Babies cry sometimes. That's what they do. If you can't stand the sound of a baby crying, then it's a good thing you don't have one. Let's hope you never have a baby. Let's hope some baby never has to suffer with you as his mother."

She burst into tears. She sobbed so intensely that the boot she was trying on dropped from her hand, so intensely that I wondered if she was faking it. Eventually her friend pulled her up by the elbow, collected her shoes and purse, and said, "Come on, let's go."

It wasn't until years later that I stopped to wonder why the woman had reacted that way. It was only then that I thought about what might have happened to her. Had she been unable to have a child, or had she lost one to stillbirth or infant death? It was only then that I thought about the gray in her life I couldn't see, instead of the black and white I saw. It was only then that I realized that I'd had no kindness for her, either.

Things are never only as they appear. My hospice patients have taught me that. There are always layers to people's lives, unseen memories under every face, every decision, every movement or lack of movement. There is always gray between the black and white.

I knocked on the door the next week at our regular visit time. Frank pulled it open and stood on the other side of the screen silently.

"Hello, Frank," I said.

He stood and stared. He didn't look angry so much as he looked empty. We waited in silence for a full minute. Then he pushed the screen door and held it open to me. I stepped in, and he turned around and walked away without speaking.

I followed him into the living room and went over to Alice's bed. She smiled and lifted her index finger, a signal that she wanted to hold my hand. As we always did, I recited the Hail Mary out loud ten times, an Our Father, and a Glory Be — a decade of the Rosary — while she mouthed the words. She closed her eyes and released her soft grip on my hand.

I turned to look at Frank. He was sitting in his recliner, watching us. He had his arms crossed on his chest and his chin low, and still he said nothing to me.

"Hi, Frank. May I sit down?"

No answer. I remained standing. "You're angry at me. I'm sorry."

Nothing.

"Frank." I hesitated. Should I go into a full explanation of what had happened? Try to justify my actions? Argue that I hadn't technically told Christy? Explain that my obligation to my patient's safety and well-being overrode his desire for secrecy? In essence, ruin the relationship we had built?

Instead I just said, "You know, I have to live in the gray, too."

He sucked his breath in and raised his head up and back. "Yes," he said slowly. "Yes, I suppose you do."

I waited another ten seconds in silence, then I picked up my bag to get ready to go.

"You can sit down," he said at last.

That there is gray in our lives, and not just in our lives but in the lives of every single person we meet, does not absolve us from having to act. It cannot prevent life from moving on, for even not moving causes ripples in the world as others move around our stillness.

Living in the gray doesn't absolve us from having to do hard things and make hard choices. If anything, it makes those choices harder.

But perhaps that's the point. It makes judgment of others harder, and therefore shaming them harder, too. When we can't shame others, it's harder to convince ourselves that they are nothing like us, or that nothing could ever happen to make us like them. It means acknowledging that any of us could be both a loving mother and a drug dealer who steals from dying patients; both of these things can be true. Any of us could be both a husband who took tender care of his family and a man who once killed someone. Any of us could be a chaplain who spends her days trying to comfort the dying and a woman who once drove a stranger to tears in the shoe department at Macy's.

Kindness is not the same as niceness, or putting our heads in the sand, or avoiding conflict. It is acknowledging that no life is as it seems on the surface. It is understanding that we never know all the layers in a life, and choosing to speak and act from that difficult gray place in all of us. Gray like an OxyContin tablet, like the hull of a scallop boat, like concrete.

JEREMIAH

He was a big man, both tall and broad. The left half of his body filled the chair; the right half seemed to be melting away. The skin on the right side of his face drooped inches down his cheek into a long flapping jowl, lips more downturned than seemed possible, and his eyelid draped across the socket. The left side of his face was set like stone — eye squinted, lip a firm, smoldering line. Anger radiated out of one side, exhaustion out of the other.

He'd recently been discharged from the hospital to this nursing home, a lovely, private, and expensive place. He was dying of something else, but the stroke was what people noticed. It left him aphasic, or no longer able to speak, and no longer able to use the right side of his body. His left side, though much less damaged, was stiff and spastic.

I talked to the nurse to try to get a sense

of who he was, since he wouldn't be able to speak to me. She didn't know him because he'd come to the nursing home for rehab after the stroke, after he lost his ability to talk. She said they didn't know how much brain damage there was. He didn't smile, make eye contact, or interact with the staff except to fight them when they tried to touch him. He was prone to rages in which he would lash out with his left arm and leg. She suspected the brain damage might be extensive.

"I wouldn't go in there," she said. "He doesn't like visitors, and I don't know what he would do."

"Okay. I'll just call his wife to give her my contact info, in case she ever needs anything from me."

These introductory phone calls can be tricky. There's a real art to them, especially when the patient is in a nursing home and the family is at home. You have to get your name and title in there fast, and then try to explain the role of the chaplain and why you're calling before they say they already have a pastor and hang up.

Sometimes spouses are wary. Sometimes they willingly share insights about their husbands' or wives' likes, dislikes, history, and faith, or want to set up a time to meet in person. Sometimes they say they don't want to talk to the chaplain. Sometimes they say they don't want to talk to the chaplain and then go on to talk for an hour and ask me to call back the next week, when they reiterate that they don't want to talk to the chaplain, talk for an hour, and ask me to call back again in a week. There are people out there with whom I have talked for hours, and I would never know them if they walked in and sat down right in front of me. Sometimes they open up right away, not because of anything I've said or done, but because they need to talk to someone, and the title "chaplain" means I am someone to talk to. One patient's husband cut me off just as I launched into my introductory spiel. "I know what a chaplain is," he said, "because I was in the service. The chaplain's the person you can tell your secrets to."

As I pulled out my phone to call this new patient's wife, the nurse stopped pouring pills into little cups and looked up at me.

"She's a nice lady, but very emotional. Kinda hysterical and in denial. She could use you, actually."

The nurse was right about the emotional part. The wife began to cry as soon as I introduced myself. She told me all about her beloved husband. His kindness, his humor, his strength. He'd played piano and had his own law practice for more than forty years. He was a good father. She said she knew that he was lashing out, but she didn't believe there was significant brain damage. She thought he was afraid, and that the nurses had jumped to conclusions. She said she knew they didn't like her and considered her husband a bully. She thought a visit from me was a great idea. She told me he loved the Bible. She thought it might be nice if I read to him. "He's so alone. Please go see him and read him a bit of Scripture," she said. "Please see him."

I told the nurse I was going in just to say hello.

"Suit yourself. Just make sure you sit far enough away so he can't grab or hit you. Take your lanyard off so he can't choke you," she said, nodding toward the ID around my neck. "Let me know when you're done in there so I don't worry."

Nursing home nurses usually ignore me, look vaguely bothered when I grab a patient chart to put in paperwork, and never, never, never ask me to check back in with them after a visit, so this made me a little nervous.

I knocked on the patient's door, walked in, and introduced myself. He glanced at me and then looked straight ahead. I told him his wife had asked that I visit and read to him. He made no sign of disagreeing, so I opened up to the book of Psalms. It's my go-to Bible book. Almost everyone who likes the Bible likes the psalms. I read it slowly, lingering over the poetry and watching him from the corner of my eye. He seemed to ignore me, but once I finished, he motioned with his good hand, like he was reaching out for the book.

"Do you want to hold the Bible?" I asked. He didn't nod, but he kept his shaking hand outstretched, kept his eyes fixed on the book, and grunted. I placed it open in his lap. "Maybe you could find your favorite passage, and I'll read it aloud."

The Bible was small, small enough to fit in my work bag along with giant files of folders and a laptop computer. The print was tiny and the paper like wisps. I could barely read it myself if the light was low. He began to use his left hand, the fingers stiff and splayed, to try to turn the pages. He couldn't really manipulate them, though, with his hand so clumsy. He slowly but too forcefully swiped at them, pushing swaths of paper back and forth, going forward and back in the book. The tissue-thin pages crumpled. He ripped some of them, grunting. Back and forth he went, slowly swiping bunches of pages. Tissue paper began drifting to the ground as pages tore away from the binding. He never lifted his eyes from his activity.

I perched on the edge of my seat and watched this. I couldn't tell if he was meaninglessly turning the pages or angrily trying to destroy the book.

"Do you have a favorite verse?" I asked tentatively. I reached out to take the damaged book from him. He roughly swatted my hand, and then continued to turn the pages. His concentration was absolute, almost palpable.

I didn't know how to end this. Even if he was looking for a particular passage, I couldn't see how he would ever find it. I didn't know how to get the Bible back from him, and I didn't know how to bring a graceful end to a process that had been going on for at least five minutes now, a very long five minutes. I considered getting the nurse, but worried that doing so would destroy whatever chance I had of making a connection with him. I was afraid of getting near enough to him to get the book back. I didn't know what to do and was embarrassed by my own uncertainty. I wanted to get out of there.

Then he stopped, grunted loudly at me,

and held the book out to me in his violently trembling hand.

I took it gingerly and looked down. The Bible, what was left of it, was open to a page in Jeremiah.

Most of the book of Jeremiah is a tough read. Jeremiah was a Hebrew prophet whose scathing critique of his people gave rise to the word "jeremiad," a long, bitter list of society's faults and predictions of its collapse. A jeremiad is not comforting.

The biblical prophets, despite what all too many people think, were not fortune-tellers. They did not predict events far in the future, and while early Christians (and some still today) liked to look for places where Jesus was foretold centuries earlier in the writings, that's not what the prophets themselves were trying to do.

The prophets were trying to tell hard truths to people who didn't want to hear it, right then and right there.

Jeremiah didn't pull any punches with his hard truths. He lived during a turbulent and devastating time for the Hebrew people. In the forty-some-odd years that he dictated his book to his scribe Baruch, he also went out and preached in public about all the sins and shortcomings of the Hebrews and the terrible things that would befall them if they continued, wrote scathing letters to the priests and elders, and did things to draw attention to his warnings (fun things like roaming the streets with a massive wooden yoke around his neck). During this span, the kingdom of Judah was invaded and collapsed, the Temple in Jerusalem was utterly destroyed, and the Babylonian Exile began, sending the Hebrew people away from the land God had promised them and into Babylon. They lost their homeland and Jewish life as they knew it. It seemed God had abandoned them and broken all His promises to them.

Jeremiah had been warning his people that disaster was imminent for years — decades — and he placed the blame squarely on their shoulders. He told the Hebrew people that they deserved all the hardships they faced. He said that the Lord had told him to say all these things.

So when my patient landed in Jeremiah, forcefully handed me the open Bible, grunted, and nodded, I had a flash of panic. Should I read it aloud, no matter what it said? What if he had landed in, say, Jeremiah, chapter 17:

Through your own fault you will lose
the inheritance I gave you.

I will enslave you to your enemies
in a land you do not know,
for you have kindled my anger,
and it will burn forever.

Or Jeremiah, chapter 4:

What are you doing, you devastated one?
Why dress yourself in scarlet
and put on jewels of gold?
Why highlight your eyes with makeup?
You adorn yourself in vain.
Your lovers despise you;
they want to kill you.

Should I flip to another page? Should I
pretend to not understand? There was no
way, I thought, that he could have meant to
land in Jeremiah.

"Do you want me to read this to you?" I
asked. For the first time he looked at me. I
thought I saw the barest nod.

I looked down at the torn and mangled
Bible now in my lap. I quickly scanned the
two lines at the top of the page.

I looked over at the man. "Is this your
favorite?" I asked, stupidly. He looked away,
so that his drooping side faced me.

I read the lines out loud.

I have loved you with an everlasting love;
I have drawn you with unfailing kindness.

Tears began to roll down his cheek, but he was quiet. I was relieved. The verse he'd landed on wasn't a blistering one. He was calm. I had the remainder of my Bible back.

And then, because I was afraid, and because my fear stopped me from being curious, I stopped reading.

"Okay!" I said, with false brightness. "Time for me to go!"

I picked up my bag and walked out.

"What in the world was going on in there?" the nurse asked.

"Oh, it was fine," I said. "I just read a little bit to him."

It was only when I got home that I read the rest of the chapter.

The LORD appeared to us in the past,
    saying:
"I have loved you with an everlasting love;
I have drawn you with unfailing kindness.
I will build you up again,
and you, Virgin Israel, will be rebuilt.
Again you will take up your timbrels
and go out to dance with the joyful.
Again you will plant vineyards
on the hills of Samaria;

the farmers will plant them
and enjoy their fruit.
There will be a day when watchmen cry out
on the hills of Ephraim,
'Come, let us go up to Zion,
to the LORD our God.' "

This is what the LORD says:
"Sing with joy for Jacob;
shout for the foremost of the nations.
Make your praises heard, and say,
'LORD, save your people, the remnant of
    Israel.'
See, I will bring them from the land of the
    north
and gather them from the ends of the earth.
Among them will be the blind and the lame,
expectant mothers and women in labor;
a great throng will return. . . .

"They will come and shout for joy on the
    heights of Zion;
they will rejoice in the bounty of the
    LORD —
the grain, the new wine and the olive oil,
the young of the flocks and herds.
They will be like a well-watered garden,
and they will sorrow no more.
Then young women will dance and be glad,
young men and old as well.

I will turn their mourning into gladness;
I will give them comfort and joy instead of
   sorrow."

Can you think of any words more comforting for a man who had lost so much? The words of God, as Jeremiah reported them, promising that in the midst of such loss, there not only could be, but would be, joy again? That there would be dancing and singing? That even old men would dance and be glad again?

These were the words he handed to me. He had spent ten minutes and untold effort to find the words he wanted to hear, and I did not read them to him.

So why? Why, even after I read the lovely verse at the top of the page?

Already on edge from the nurse's warnings, and more so as he'd destroyed the Bible, I'd seen JEREMIAH at the top of the page and assumed the worst. I'd forgotten that even though God had decried the behavior of the people of Judah, he had also promised that their suffering would not last forever. Through Jeremiah, the Lord had promised the people that they would return home, that they would survive. And they did. In fact, some scholars argue that it was during the Babylonian Exile that the Jewish people really became Jewish. That was when Judaism developed its revolutionary and defining belief in monotheism. Unable to perform animal sacrifices, which could only be done in the Temple in Jerusalem, the Jews began to study the Torah in earnest, and the rabbinic tradition was born. Worship in newly formed local synagogues began and included singing, prayers, and readings from the Torah, which are the hallmarks of Jewish worship today. In these ways and more, the Babylonian Exile made the Jewish people more deeply who they were. I had focused only on the suffering, forgetting that something wonderful was born of it. I'd forgotten that even in the midst of Jeremiah's screeds, God promised His people comfort. He promised that although they might suffer, they would never be destroyed. He promised that even if they turned away from him, he would never stop loving them.

I had been on edge, yes. But I had also already made up my mind about this man about whom I knew almost nothing. I had assumed that he did not know what he was doing and that the page he landed on was a mistake or a coincidence. I had judged him incompetent based on a few grunts, some spastic movements, and the nurse's report.

I didn't see the kind husband, the success-
ful lawyer, the doting grandfather. A man
who very well might have a biblical passage
so dear to him that he would destroy a Bible
to find it.

His wife had not asked me to comfort
him. She had asked me to see him. In that,
I failed. I'd visited him, but I had not actually seen him. I hadn't been able to see past
his stroke-damaged body.

The desire to be seen and known and ac-
cepted for who one really is comes up time
and again with my families and patients. It
must be hard when other people's perception of your body does not match up with
who you know yourself to be, and when
people judge you based only on that body.
It must be hard when those around you
refuse to accept you as you identify yourself,
finding you frightening, or something to
pity.

"This might sound crazy to you," another
patient said very slowly as she carefully re-
arranged some flowers in a vase. Sally had
worked for decades as a florist, had been
happily married, raised four children, played
bridge on Tuesdays and Bunko on Thurs-
days at the library, liked nothing better than
a cruise in the Caribbean in the middle of
the harsh, wet Rhode Island winter. "I'm

actually Joan of Arc. Reincarnated."

"Ahh," I said.

"Do you think I'm crazy?" She stopped fiddling with the flowers and looked directly at me.

"No."

"Why not?"

"Half the world believes in reincarnation. Who am I to say it isn't true?"

She sighed deeply. "That's a relief." She sighed again. "I can't even begin to tell you how much of a relief that is. Thank you."

Her son was concerned. "Mom told me that she told you about her Joan of Arc thing?" he said one day.

"She did," I answered.

"Thanks for going along with it. She's not really crazy, you know. We have no idea where this comes from. She's been saying it for years. God, maybe decades. Long before she got sick. It meant a lot to her, that you didn't think she was crazy."

One of the benefits of having actually gone crazy myself is that "crazy" doesn't bother me. That experience changed my definition and understanding of crazy completely.

The bigger benefit, though, is that I'm not so quick to reject ideas of what might be possible. I suppose that's why people take dissociative drugs like ketamine recreationally in the first place — to expand their minds. I guess in that sense it worked for me. Despite all the trauma and pain it brought me, it also left me willing to entertain just about any idea people throw my way. Not that I don't have my own set of beliefs and principles, but I can usually see someone else's point and the logic behind their beliefs, no matter how unusual, and not be concerned or threatened by it.

"I don't know why she holds on to that idea," Sally's son said, perplexed. "Why in the world would she say such a thing?"

Because maybe she really is the reincarnation of Joan of Arc, I thought but didn't say.

Now, I didn't necessarily believe that Sally was Joan. Of course, there was no definitive proof she wasn't, either. How could you prove it? It would be like trying to prove there are no green aliens. You can't prove a negative.

A much more interesting question to ask would have been "What does it mean to be the reincarnation of Joan of Arc? How does that affect your life?"

I never got to ask that, though. Sally never again brought up reincarnation, or her identity, although there were plenty of chances to. It seemed that it was just important to her that I know and accept that she was who she believed herself to be.

Who do you believe yourself to be? It's a strange question, right? But trying to answer it honestly tells a person so much about themselves.

When I was sick, back in the days of flip phones, I put a banner message on my home screen so that I saw it every time I opened the phone.

It said, YOU ARE CAPABLE.

At the time, I was not capable. I was not capable of holding down a job. I was not capable of taking care of a baby. I was not even capable of taking care of myself.

But I needed to believe, despite all outward appearances and the circumstances in which I found myself, that I was capable at my very core, even if I was not capable right then. I needed to be reminded of it, all day long.

But I also needed to keep it a secret. I didn't write it on a note to pin above the kitchen sink or on the bathroom mirror, as I often do with things I need to remember.

I didn't want anyone to see that message for two reasons. First, I didn't want anyone to know that I needed to be reminded of it; I didn't want pity. Second, I was afraid that someone would tell me it wasn't actually true. I didn't want someone to say, in the slow, soothing, insulting voice people often adopted when speaking to me then, that I had once been a capable person, but that it was no longer the case, and that I was now officially and forevermore an incapable person. I was afraid that the ketamine and the psychosis might have changed the very deepest part of me, that my basic identity had been destroyed. That I suddenly, at the age of thirty-one, had become no one at all.

Are we created by our experiences? Can our deepest self be destroyed by what happens in this life? Or do we have some sort of unchanging, essential soul?

When I walked in, John put down the book he was reading. It was a history of the very earliest years of the colony of Massachusetts. Many of the events it described had taken place in the area where we were sitting, on Buzzards Bay.

"Glad I wasn't a Pilgrim on a day like today," he said.

I knew what he meant. Winter along the southern coast of Massachusetts is brutal. It's gray every single day, depressing by two thirty in the afternoon and dark at four. It is wet. So wet. The mist off the ocean freezes into little salty ice balls that the wind drives

into your skin. The frozen mist coats everything — the windows, the trees, your face
and eyes — with sticky gray salt. Some days
you never warm up, even inside with central
heat and wool socks.

"Can you imagine landing here four
hundred years ago?" I said. "And there's
nothing? Nowhere to get inside, nowhere to
warm up, nowhere to buy food?"

"Would have been awful. Just the beach
and that boat you'd been stuck on for
months already. Couldn't get out of the
wet." He nodded gravely.

"Those Pilgrims were tough people. I
would have turned around and gone back.
They were much tougher than me."

He cocked his head to the side and looked
at me carefully. "You talk about being tough
as though it's a good thing," he said finally.

I had to think for a second. "Yeah. I guess
I do think it's a good thing. I guess I wish I
was tougher."

"No you don't." He looked away and
waved his hand.

"I don't?" I asked.

"No. Toughness makes people mean.
You're lucky you don't have to be tough."
His face was weathered and lined; his hands
were thick, meaty paws; his dark brown eyes

searched my face from under deeply hooded brows.

"But toughness makes you strong. That's what I wish. That I was strong."

"You're so wrong. They're not the same at all, being tough and being strong."

"No?"

"Nope. They're opposites."

"How so?"

"You have to be tough *because* you're not strong. That's how it works. I was tough. Didn't have a choice. But it wasn't something I wanted. I'll tell you the truth: You're lucky if you don't have to become tough. You can stay who you really are. Nobody's born tough. Something makes you that way. Being tough makes you mean. It's better if you can stay kind. Nobody should want to be tough."

"What made you tough?"

He looked at me for a long time. "Life."

He'd gone off to war in the Pacific as a newly married man. While there, his wife had their first child, a little girl. He met his daughter for the first time on leave, when she was a toddler.

"Then I went back," he said. "I thought about that baby every day, and my wife every day. I would close my eyes and I could feel myself back there. I could hear them and see them and feel them. It's what got me through it. Just remembering them.

"She used to write to me almost every day, but then the letters started to come less and less. I thought she was busy with the baby, or that it was getting harder to get the letters to us. I never suspected anything.

"So when that letter came, I just snapped. She didn't love me anymore. She'd met someone else, and she was leaving me.

"She included a picture of me holding my little girl.

"You know you hear about 'Dear John' letters? It was literally a Dear John letter. I read it squatting there in the dirt. I threw it on the ground. Then I stood up and walked into the jungle. I wanted to kill someone. My officer called after me but he didn't stop me. He knew he couldn't. I walked out to where I knew there were some Japs hiding. And I killed them."

We sat in silence.

"I didn't see my daughter again for a long time. By then she was a big girl. She didn't know me, and she didn't love me. But why would she? I was a stranger to her. Hell, I was a stranger to myself. That's what being tough does. It makes you a stranger."

When I first started working in hospice, someone told me this: In most of life, you can be weak inside and get through by putting on a tough outer shell. But if you work in hospice, you have to stay soft on the outside. So in order to stand up straight, you have to have a spine of steel. Two ways to go through the world, two ways to deal with the loss that is an inevitable experience in life — with a hard shell or with a rock-solid backbone.

When I was still a hospital chaplain, a nurse called me one afternoon to the neonatal intensive care unit. A baby was dying.

She'd been born premature and very, very small, and it had seemed at first that she would survive. But then, in a galloping cascade of crises, she'd gone from surprisingly hardy to barely surviving in just an hour. It can happen like that.

While the doctors and nurses worked on the baby, I sat with the mother in one of the little windowless rooms filled with couches and boxes of tissues that most patients and visitors don't even know hospitals have. This was the mother's first pregnancy that had gone beyond the first trimester. She told me she'd had twins, and the boy had already died. She'd had preeclampsia. She was forty-three. She didn't think there would be any more children.

When there was nothing else the medical

team could do, a nurse came and got us.

Back on the unit, the baby had been wrapped in a warm blanket. The doctor handed her to the mother. For the first time, she got to see her daughter's face without tubes in the mouth and nose, without an IV in her scalp.

The woman said nothing for a long time, did not cry or ask questions. "Thank you," she said to the tiny baby in her arms. "Thank you for making me your mommy."

The three of us sat together for a long time in the corner of the neonatal intensive care unit — the baby, her mother, and me.

"I always wanted to be a mother," the woman said suddenly. "I became a mother when they were born."

"Yes," I said.

"I'm still a mother, even though they're gone. I'll always be a mother, no matter what else happens. They gave me that."

The things you lose do shape who you become. There's no getting around that. But the losses don't obliterate what came before. The loss of that mother's two babies did not negate the fact that she had become a mother and that she would remain a mother after their deaths. My stroke patient's loss of language did not negate his years as a father, husband, lawyer, piano player.

Sometimes the pain of loss is so great that an outer shell seems like the only way to protect our souls, a shell so tough we no longer recognize ourselves. But we are still there. Everything we were is still there. It's just hidden from sight. Sometimes it's even hidden from ourselves.

When I was sick, and for many, many years afterward, I desperately wanted to go back in time. I wanted to go back to being the person I was before I got sick. I missed that woman, I missed who I was — her mind, her body, her spiritual life, her beliefs about herself and the world. I wanted her back. I wanted to be her again. I thought she was gone forever. Obliterated.

But it doesn't work that way. I couldn't go back to being who I was then. But the person I'd been then wasn't gone, either.

Nature doesn't work that way. A tree puts out new, tender growth every spring. Those leaves inevitably die, but the rings of the tree's trunk are always there, deep inside, from its very first spring. Some rings are thick, when life is easy and rain plentiful. Some are so narrow they can barely be seen, when the tree is struggling to stay alive. But all the rings are still there.

A barnacle grows by accretion, its shell getting thicker and thicker with every passing day, protecting the tiny fleshy body that first attached itself to something hard. That you can no longer see that body doesn't mean that the barnacle isn't alive inside its shell.

Living things continue to develop until the moment they die, whether or not anyone else recognizes it. There's no losing who you once were, but there's no going back, either. There is only becoming.

Do we have an essential soul, or is our identity at the mercy of what happens to us? The answer seems to be both at the same time. We are becoming who we already are up until the moment we die.

Even after terrible things happen to us, we are still becoming who we are. Like the Hebrews of Jeremiah's time, who were still becoming Jews despite their enormous suffering and loss.

Tree or barnacle: There are two ways to grow, to respond to the inevitable losses and traumas of life. Two ways to become who you always were.

BORN, AND BORN AGAIN, AND AGAIN

"You know, I'm not afraid to die," Louise whispered as I read a psalm to her. I put the book down.

"You're not?"

"No. I never have been. That's not what it is."

I waited. I could tell something was coming, because Louise had never talked like this before.

Our previous visits had been what I would call "faith sharing," for lack of a better term. Louise had been born to Italian immigrant parents and raised Catholic, and she and her husband, now dead some thirty years, had raised their seven children Catholic. Louise lived with her son Ed, who was now the pastor of a nondenominational evangelical church, and her doting daughter-in-law Irene. One of them was usually there when I visited, and I'd listen to them talk about their faith and what it meant to them. Then they'd sing hymns, and Louise would always join in, and she'd smile when they read her favorite passages from the Bible. If Louise was feeling up to it, she might talk a little bit about the years when her children were small. Ed would chime in about the trouble he and his brothers used to get into. Then there would be more hymn singing, more talking about how very good God is, speculation about what Heaven would be like. The tone was always unremittingly cheerful.

This time, it was just Louise and me. She'd asked for her favorite psalm.

After a minute, she let out a deep, shuddering sigh and just the hint of a moan.

"Do you want —" I began, but she cut me off.

"My children aren't saved. Five of them aren't saved. It's all I pray about. I can't die until I know they're saved. I can't leave them. They aren't saved. Do you understand?"

I did, because I had heard this before. I had seen this pain before, from a dozen other parents.

Louise was referring to the particular evangelical Christian belief about needing to be "born again" in order to be saved and

123

therefore gain entrance to Heaven after death.

If you don't share this belief, or aren't familiar with it, put yourself, if you can, in Louise's place for a moment. You're dying, and you believe you're saved — that you are going to Heaven and you are going to meet Jesus, whom you love with all your heart. But some of your children are not going to Heaven, at least as of now. You love these children with all your heart, too. You carried them in your body and nursed them with your breasts and washed their little bodies and put Band-Aids on their knees and cooked them dinner every night for almost twenty years. You cried with them when they were rejected by friends and felt your heart leap when they hit their first home run and picked out their voice in the chorus concert. You watched them grow and felt your love for them expand. You love them still as they go through, and sometimes struggle with, life. You love them more than your own life, and maybe, secretly, even more than you love Jesus. You are told that this is how God the Father loves you. Like a parent. When you doubt God's love, you remember that God loves you like a mother or father, like you love your own children.

But you also believe that this God will let

your babies suffer forever. You believe they will go to Hell because they are not saved. You have done all you can to help these children get saved, and they aren't interested. They have their own faiths, or no faith at all. You're dying, and in your belief system, when you die you'll never see them again. Not only will they be lost to you forever, but they will suffer. That makes God a monster, and parenting monstrous, and love a lie.

But you cannot admit this. You cannot admit that this belief, the bedrock of your faith — and for someone like Louise, of your social and familial world — is shaking you to your core. Except to the chaplain, when your children aren't in the room.

If I were Louise, I wouldn't want to die, either.

There were so many times, when talking to people like her, that I wanted to shout, "That's only one interpretation among many within Christianity! This is not the only way, or even the most common or oldest way, to understand salvation! There are other ways, different ways, to answer these questions!"

But that's not what a chaplain does. A chaplain isn't there to convince you to change your faith. She isn't there to give a history or theology lesson. She isn't there to convince you to believe what she believes.

A chaplain is there to help you figure out what you believe, what gives you comfort, the meaning of your life, who God is to you. Not to her.

So I learned to bite my lip and to ask, "What was it like? The day you were saved?" I learned to ask that question from another patient.

Eleanor was a tiny woman, not more than five feet tall and less than a hundred pounds. She was dying of rectal cancer, which was embarrassing and humiliating for her. She was very social by nature, and proud, and she had loved flirting with men and talking with her friends. But now she was so terrified of the possibility of having an accident that she stayed close to her bathroom, taking all her meals in her bedroom in her assisted-living facility.

Her room was dominated by a queen-size bed with a flowered comforter that she had brought from home, and that seemed to swallow her up whenever I saw her lying in it, which was more and more the case as time went on. But usually she sat in her light blue recliner, next to a clear Rubbermaid storage chest stuffed full of yarn that she was no longer able to knit because her fingers were too arthritic. The shade was always drawn on the one window in her room because she couldn't see the television when the shade was up and it was too difficult for her to raise and lower it by herself in the middle of the day.

Eleanor had outlived three husbands. She had no children. Her toenails caused her enormous pain, and her dentures clattered in her shrunken mouth. She was so angry to still be alive.

You learn working in hospice that a person can, in fact, live too long.

Once, after I knocked on the door and said hello, she waved her hand dismissively, looked away, and said with bitterness, "I know who you are, so just say your bit and go." Usually, though, she smiled when I knocked and asked me to come in and talk, and offered me her uneaten lunch tray.

She talked mostly about her late husbands, her sister, and the beauty of her farm. She was a lifelong Southern Baptist, she said, but she didn't talk about her faith or her spiritual life, even when I prompted her, and only ever mentioned her church to say angrily that they no longer visited her. She didn't have a favorite verse from Scripture, unlike almost every other Baptist I've known. To be honest, I was never sure that she really wanted my visits, or if she was just politely putting up with me, as well-reared Southern women do. But one day, in the midst of talking about I don't remember what, she mentioned the day she was saved.

I asked her to tell me more about it.

"Tell you about what?"

"What happened when you were saved. What did it feel like? How did you know it had happened?"

"I can close my eyes and feel it again," she said. Her body, which she always held tensely — arms pinned to her lap, legs together, stooped forward in the chair instead of leaning back — relaxed into the recliner. The grimace and forehead furrows melted. "I was at a revival meeting. Lots of people were going up to the front of the tent and being saved. I'd seen it happen before, the preacher putting out the call. But I never felt like I wanted to go up there. That day seemed no different. But then. Then. I never really understood what happened, but when I walked out of that tent, suddenly the leaves were so green on the trees. I don't know how I had never noticed that green before. It was like the color on the whole world was turned up. I could see every single blade of grass. I could hear every bird sing. I could feel each ray of the sun on my skin. And I knew it right then, that Jesus loved me and died for me and I was saved because he loved me so much. I knew he was the Lord. Everything was so beautiful, so alive. The whole world had changed. I didn't know how I hadn't seen it before. Everything changed because I was saved. Or maybe I was saved because everything changed."

It instantly became my favorite question to ask of my evangelical patients: *What was it like, the day you were saved?* Every single one of them had almost the same story. Everything looked different and sounded different, even the air felt different. The world was made anew for them. "I couldn't believe how alive the world was. And I had never noticed before." Truly, they felt born again, not just in their faith but in the world itself. They experienced a new creation.

Just asking them to remember and relive that day — to close their eyes and see what they saw, smell what they smelled, hear what they heard — could bring even the most despondent patient joy.

I'd ask them what remembering that day told them about God. Sometimes, pondering that question would bring about a new understanding of their current situation. Sometimes it would make their current spiritual questions even more puzzling.

Always, however, they were left in wonder at how nothing in the physical world had changed but their own perception of it. That was enough to change everything. Always, I was left in wonder that such a massive shift could happen in less than a second. It seems miraculous.

For many years, I wanted change. At the same time, I despised the changes that I felt had been forced on me by that fateful surgery.

I wanted to change what had happened when my first baby was born so badly, I could taste it. For a long time I was convinced I'd brought it on myself, by eating too much ice cream. I was ten days overdue when he was born. Every night after his due date my husband and I had driven out into the Iowa countryside to a little shop that sold homemade ice cream. I loved those drives in the June dusk through the knee-high corn, zigzagging against the hills and the lightning bugs just beginning to blink. I can close my eyes and still taste the ice cream melting in my mouth while we watched our enormous baby's arms and legs bulge out through my belly when he moved, like a scene from *Alien.* Was it the ice cream that made him grow so big — so big he got stuck in the birth canal, leading to the C-section, leading to the failure of the epidural, leading to the ketamine, leading to the psychosis? If I had just not eaten that ice cream, could I have made it all not happen? Had I just been too happy?

In my mind, I used to go through every second of the days and hours that led up to his birth, trying to understand what I could have changed to fix it all, to avoid the fear and terror that raced through my body and head every waking moment, to get back those lost years.

I wanted the chance to do it again, to be a new mother again, to drink in his baby smell and kiss his baby head and actually remember it.

I wanted my memories, the memories lost to posttraumatic stress disorder and dissociation. The only way I could seem to cope with this overwhelming longing was by perseverating about what I could have changed.

When I listened to my evangelical patients' day-I-was-saved stories, I understood in a visceral way the connection between change and salvation. It seemed that change was the only thing that could save me from the pain I was in.

Sarah, another woman living in an assisted-living facility, wanted change, too. Sarah was as aloof and reserved as Eleanor was angry. She loved the Rosary, a repetitive and meditative prayer that often leads to a deep state of contemplation, and we always said several decades of the Rosary together. She barely spoke, however, during our first few meetings, and would only glance at me fleetingly before looking out the window at the fountain in the garden just outside her rooms. She always asked me to return, though, so I did. Slowly, over the course of several visits, she began to open up just a little.

Sarah never joined in on any of the activities the facility sponsored, staying in her room all day instead. That, of course, was her right. All of us — the hospice team and her children — thought that it was also her desire.

Until one day I showed up at her apartment with a string of fat beads around my neck.

"I like your necklace," she said shyly.

The facility was hosting a Mardi Gras party in the dining room, and the activities director had bedecked me as I passed through, I explained.

"I heard it," she replied. "I wish I had gone."

I jumped up from my seat and told her it was still going on. I offered to wheel her down the long hall to the party.

"Oh no," she said, and her hands flew up to her face. "I couldn't. I wouldn't know what to do, or what to say. I would just be so embarrassed. Oh, no. No. No."

I sat back down, asked if she was sure. Yes, she was sure. She was just too shy to go, she explained.

"I often wonder," she said haltingly, "what it would be like to have friends and go to parties and be part of it all. I wonder what my life would have been like if I hadn't been so shy all the time."

Over the next few visits, it became very clear that Sarah was not aloof and reserved. She wasn't choosing not to participate and socialize. In fact, she desperately wanted to be a part of the bingo games and craft classes, and she longed to go on the mystery bus trips and to holiday parties. She just felt too shy to do so.

She would sometimes see the exuberant activities director leading a conga line of dancers down the hallway and pray that they would stop in front of her door and ask her to come out and join them. But the conga line never made it that far.

She always left her door wide open and sat directly in front of it in hopes that someone would walk by and say hello, and that perhaps they could become friends that way. But that never happened.

Sarah's room was in the worst spot possible in the entire facility for that sort of interaction. Hers was the last apartment at the end of a very long hallway branching off from the main living room. So while she could see all the fun, no one ever walked past her door.

When I shared Sarah's predicament at our hospice team meeting, we hatched a plan. We'd set up several volunteers to come visit Sarah every week. Together, they could go to whatever activity was going on at the time, so Sarah wouldn't have to brave the living room alone. The social worker would work with her on conversation skills. Beth, the RN case manager, would advocate to have Sarah moved into a new apartment, one that was closer to the center of activity where she could feel like she was a part of things.

Sarah's children supported the plan, and Sarah herself was excited and apprehensively looking forward to the changes. The first were easy to put into place. The volunteer coordinator sent over three of her best, most skilled volunteers that week. The social worker started visiting weekly.

The move, however, was going to take some time and doing. Sarah had to wait until someone in a more centrally located apartment moved out. Beth had to convince the facility's administration that this was a necessary move. After a couple of months, the day arrived. An apartment just two doors down from the dining room, right in the center of all the excitement, was hers.

But Sarah refused to move.

I visited her a few days later and asked what had happened.

While the new apartment would have placed her right in the middle of the building, she explained, it meant giving up her view of the garden and fountain. The garden she watched all winter, waiting for the barest trace of green in March, and all spring as the bulbs burst from the ground and the crabapple tree erupted into pink blossoms, and all summer as the roses bloomed, and all fall as the leaves on the hickory tree just beyond the garden turned the sky to electric yellow. The fountain she had been contemplating every day for the five years she had lived there, as she said her Rosary.

She wanted a change, but she would have to give all that up to get it. No other apartment in the facility had that view. She was faced with a dilemma: the quiet contemplation she had known all her life, or the excitement and friendship she had craved for just as long.

Was it that she was afraid of changing? I asked.

She looked out the window and played with the rosary beads in her lap. No, that was not it.

A few days before Sarah had been set to change apartments, she saw her mother at the foot of her bed. She saw her there frequently lately, but this time her mother was standing with a young woman whom she didn't know. They were holding hands. They were smiling at Sarah and nodding. She didn't know what it meant.

The day before she was supposed to move, her daughter had come to help her pack up. They began to look through one of her old albums, where they came across a very old photograph.

"That's when I recognized the strange woman. It was my birth mother."

"Your birth mother?"

"Yes. She had died in childbirth when I

was born. I never met her. My father remarried when I was two, and it was my stepmother who raised me. She was the only mother I knew. But I have one photograph of my birth mother in her wedding gown. When I saw the picture I realized the stranger was my birth mother. She and my mother were holding hands at the foot of my bed.

"I suddenly realized that I have been this way since I was born. I have been shy every day of my life. They were telling me it was okay. That I didn't have to be ashamed of never fitting in, of always being on the edge of things. That they loved me just the way I am.

"I like going to bingo with the volunteers, but I can't give up my garden. It's who I am, who I've always been. I don't need to change that."

Sarah's choice was not to change. Instead, she let go of the regret for her nature that she had been carrying around. She let go of the regret for a life she didn't lead and embraced the one she had. She made small changes that made her happy now, but she didn't need to change her past.

I had been focused on changing my past, but it doesn't work that way, of course. No one can go back in time to change what happened, unless you're Marty McFly or Doctor Who, and it didn't always go so well for them, either. You cannot change your past, and you cannot change yourself in the past.

I couldn't change any piece of what happened. All I could change was how I saw it.

The radical, joyful, healing change my born-again patients experienced was not a change of circumstance or past experiences. It was a change of vision. A change of insight, of understanding who they really were — a person so beloved by God that they were saved, not by what they did but simply because they were. The world was not born anew, but the way they saw it was. The leaves had always been green; they just had never noticed how beautiful green is. Countless rays of sunshine had landed on their skin all their lives; they had just never felt what was always there.

Was it the awareness of a world so alive that made them realize they were loved? Or was it the awareness that they were loved that made the world born again? It was always a bit of chicken-and-egg when they tried to puzzle it out.

And yet their radical new understanding hadn't prevented further pain from entering my patients' lives, even after they'd been saved. It didn't prevent Louise's intense crisis of faith over the unsaved children she feared she wouldn't see again, provoked by a God she believed had loved her enough to save her. It didn't prevent Eleanor from feeling abandoned by everyone who had ever loved her, including God, as she hobbled alone from recliner to toilet and back again, one hundred times a day.

Even the kind of momentous change in perspective that my patients believed was enough to save them for eternity on the day they were saved wasn't enough change to get them through life on earth. More change, ongoing change, is required of us all, it seems, as long as we're alive, even if we've been saved, even if we already know that we are lovable.

I'm not a theologian, or a preacher, or a priest. I cannot comment on and do not pretend to be able to tease out the intricacies of soteriology — the theories of salvation. But I do know that, on this human plane, the knot of change, salvation, and love cannot be untangled.

If you want to be saved from your present suffering, you must be willing to change and be changed in the present.

That change can be tangible — leaving an

abusive relationship, going back to school, moving down the hallway in an assisted-living facility.

But it can also be a change in perception. This, in fact, is the harder change.

A change of perception to knowing you are enough, and have been since birth, to seeing a world suffused in love and swimming in beauty, despite loneliness, despite pain, despite illness, loss, trauma, and even atrocity — now that's hard. That seems impossible. Yet it happens, again and again, and again.

LOVE AND OTHER
REAL THINGS

There was no mistaking the medicine woman when she stopped just a few feet inside the doorway and put down her bags. Not because she was dressed in traditional tribal clothing. She wasn't. She wore khakis and a button-down shirt. It was that you couldn't help but look at her, lean in to her, listen to her. She changed the feeling in the air. Her eyes traveled the room, gazing briefly at each of us. Another woman, younger, walked in behind her, carrying more bags.

I smiled at my patient, Linda. Her hair, a steel-gray crew cut bisected by a shiny raised scar that zigzagged from her ear all the way across and down her scalp, made spikes against the half-dozen pillows that propped her up in bed. Her hugely swollen hands clutched the white hospital sheets. Her eyes were enormous. They flew from the medicine woman to me, back to the medicine woman and then to me again.

Linda's partner, Kathy, shut off the television and stood up heavily. Barb the social worker put down her pen and, in one swift motion, shuffled her stack of papers into a neat pile and flipped them over. She walked over to the medicine woman and held out her hand.

"Thank you so much. We're so grateful you came."

Linda was dying of brain cancer. She was fifty-five. She had undergone every therapy there was, but none stopped the march of the aggressive tumor that wound its way through her brain. At her hospice admission she'd asked to see the chaplain and said that it was urgent.

When I met Linda the next day, she'd lain listlessly in bed while Kathy jumped up from the recliner, gave me a huge, body-swallowing hug, and thanked me for coming. "Sit right here," she'd said as she removed a towel from the back of the recliner. "She's been waiting for you." She picked up a stack of magazines. "I'm going to go check in with the nurse and give you two some privacy."

"No!" Linda rasped. She seemed to rouse herself from a trance. It was the first thing she had said since I'd walked in, though her eyes hadn't left me. Her eyes slowly, slowly shifted to where Kathy stood. "Please stay. I want you to stay. There's nothing I can't say in front of you."

Kathy paused and looked at me.

"That's fine, if that's what Linda wants," I said.

Kathy seemed unsure, caught mid-motion. But in a moment, she regained her steely composure, put her magazines on the dresser, and asked me to sit in the recliner. She was back with a folding chair before I was even settled.

Kathy introduced herself as Linda's friend.

"She's my best friend," Linda corrected, in her slow, spacey cadence. "She's my everything."

Kathy reached out to grab her hand, and looked down to hide the blush and enormous smile that spread across her face. "Why don't you tell Kerry why you wanted to see the chaplain?" she prodded.

"Will you do it, please?" said Linda.

And as so often happened with Linda and Kathy, Kathy did all the talking.

Kathy explained that Linda was Cherokee, and that she needed to see a medicine man or woman. An evil spirit was attached to her, and the only way to remove it was with a special ceremony that only such a shaman could perform. Could I help? Could I find such a person?

One of the many things a hospice chaplain does is help connect patients and families with the clergy of their chosen religion. Some people have been members of a church or synagogue for a long time and don't need my help with this. Many people, however, do. They may have grown up Catholic but haven't been to Mass in decades. Others may identify culturally and ethnically as Jewish but haven't uttered a prayer since their bar or bat mitzvah. Sometimes in the face of death, the desire for the prayers and rituals of one's youth comes crashing back, often to the surprise, sheepish embarrassment, or confusion of the dying.

I had a thick printout of local clergy people in each of the towns I covered, in almost every religious tradition you could think of. But I did not know a medicine person, or even how to find one.

"The admissions nurse said you could help us. That you'd be able to find someone," Kathy said. She sat on the edge of her chair, rested her forearms on the bed, and leaned all the way toward me. Her forehead creased. There was a crack in her otherwise cheerful, efficient manner.

Linda had been steadfastly staring at Kathy's face as she spoke, but her head now swiveled toward me. She fixed her large, slightly drooping eyes on me. Very slowly and very quietly she said, "I have to get rid of it before I die. It's been attached to me since I was a little girl. It's bad, and it's made bad things happen to me. I've been through so many bad things because of it. I'm afraid of what will happen to me if I die and it's still in me."

I said I would try.

I didn't believe in Linda's evil spirit. I don't really believe in demons or spirit possession or anything like that. As I got to know Linda, I came to think of her evil spirit not as an actual, "real" thing but as a metaphor for the abuse she'd endured in her life, and the cascading effects that abuse had. I believed that she did indeed have darkness and pain in her soul, but that it stemmed from trauma and depression. I thought the ritual could be cathartic. It could be a tangible experience of letting go of her pain. But a real evil spirit, a being separate from Linda that had somehow invaded her soul or attached itself to her person? No. I did not believe in that.

145

I always try to understand and empathize with the beliefs of my patients. Usually, I truly can see why they believe what they do, and their beliefs are beautiful to me. But sometimes, I just can't buy in all the way. This was one of those times.

But a chaplain is not there to doubt, or to act upon her own religious beliefs. A chaplain's job is to help the patient meet his or her spiritual needs, whatever they may be. Even finding someone to remove an evil spirit.

Linda and Kathy had met on an Internet dating site. Just a few weeks later, Linda moved all the way across the country to be with Kathy. They were happy. Happy for the first time in her life, Linda said. A little over a year later, she was diagnosed with aggressive and terminal brain cancer. Kathy had taken care of her at home as long as she could, but eventually she couldn't afford to take any more time off from work. There was no one else to care for Linda, and they didn't have the money to pay for home care. It had just about crushed Kathy, that Linda had to move to a nursing home. But here they were.

Kathy spent every moment possible with Linda. She came to the nursing home each morning before dawn, leaving from there for her job as an elementary school teacher and returning directly from work. She'd hung up pictures and posters to decorate the little room, and at Christmas she set up a tiny artificial tree in the corner. She brought in Linda's favorite foods, and boxes of doughnuts for the staff. She did much of the patient care when she was there, feeding, bathing, and repositioning Linda in bed. They watched TV together. They held hands. They spent a lot of time just looking at each other.

When I visited Linda alone, she watched me carefully with her huge eyes. She talked in a raspy whisper, so that I had to sit very close to the bed and lean my head in. She talked about her hope that we would find a medicine person who could make her better.

Remarkably, I never heard a word of bitterness from her about her diagnosis, her abusive childhood, her failed marriage, or her estranged children. I didn't actually hear much about these topics at all. She referred to them briefly and obliquely, with few details, even when I asked directly about them. Instead, Linda talked about what Heaven would be like, why she believed there was an evil spirit attached to her, where it came from and what it felt like, and what it would feel like to be rid of it. We talked about movies and television and music. She talked about how much she loved Kathy, how her life had changed when they met, and how no one in her life had ever, ever cared for her the way Kathy had over the months of her illness. She didn't understand how someone could care for her the way Kathy had.

Kathy was a whirlwind of a caregiver and patient advocate, what any chaplain would hope for for her patients. At the beginning of Linda's time on hospice, Kathy was hopeful that somehow something would change, and that Linda would not die. Even when we sat together in the nursing home, with Linda declining in front of her, she read about cyber knives and radiation seeds. I think, though she never said it, that she hoped the medicine person would be able to remove not only the evil spirit but the cancer. Because all Kathy wanted was more time with Linda.

In front of Linda, Kathy was upbeat, consoling, in control. But when she called me privately, from a supply closet at work, she was barely able to hold herself together. It was from Kathy that I learned how Linda had once fought off a mountain lion attack with just her bare hands, how she'd saved a man's life by dragging him from a burning car, getting severely burned herself in the ordeal. She had the scars all over her body to prove it. As Linda got weaker and more confused and spent more of her day asleep, Kathy shared more of the remarkable stories Linda had told her.

"Have you ever known of a person as amazing as her?" she asked once. "It just doesn't seem possible for one person to have done so many amazing things."

I continued my search. I called all the tribes in the area, looking for a lead. I called anthropology and religion professors at universities. I waded through Web page after Web page. There were lots of people out there who'd been inspired by Native American spiritual practice to call themselves shamans, but actual, traditionally trained Native American medicine people were hard to find. One afternoon, while I was reporting on the latest in my quest, Kathy suggested that I reach out to Wilma Mankiller, the famed Cherokee leader. "I think if she understood that her own daughter needed help, she would fly out here herself, or at least find someone who could," she said in exasperation.

"What do you mean?" I asked. I looked at Linda, who just looked back at me with those enormous, quiet eyes of hers. Her face had no expression.

"Well, hasn't Linda told you?" Kathy said. "She isn't just Cherokee. She's the daughter of Wilma Mankiller herself. But Wilma was forced to give her away for adoption when she was born, because Wilma was just a teenager. Linda, haven't you told her? Tell her, Linda. Tell her who you really are."

Linda and I looked at each other. I raised my eyebrows. No response.

One day Barb the social worker called with good news. She had found a medicine woman who was also a university professor. She was willing to meet our patient and to perform a healing ritual that would release Linda's evil spirit. She declined any compensation, even for her travel expenses. She was coming Friday.

I went in to see Linda the next day to see what she thought of this development. She was dozing when I walked in. When I touched her shoulder, she opened her eyes and smiled her slow, soporific smile. But when I mentioned the upcoming visit, she bit her lip and fat tears began rolling down her cheeks. She clutched my hand.

"What's wrong?" I asked.

"I'm afraid," she whispered.

"Of what?"

"Of this. I don't know how to stop this," she said.

"Do you really want to do this, Linda?" I asked her. "Is this what you actually want? Because if you don't, just say it. You don't have to do this, if it's not what you really want."

"I don't know what else to do," she said. "I have to."

That was how we found ourselves in the little room — Linda, Kathy, Barb, and me — when the medicine woman arrived.

Linda's droopy eyes were suddenly wide open. The medicine woman asked her for her full name and where she was born.

"And what clan are you?" she asked.

Linda's mouth opened just a bit, but she said nothing. After a few seconds, Kathy bent over her and repeated the question.

Linda looked at me, and I nodded. She remained silent for another few seconds. Finally she licked her lips and whispered, "Owl."

Now the medicine woman was silent.

"There is no Owl clan in the Cherokee Nation," she said at last.

"She has a brain tumor," Kathy quickly said. "She's confused and forgetful. I can call someone to find out."

"No, that's okay," the medicine woman said slowly. She looked at Linda carefully. "I'll need everyone to leave the room now."

"I can't stay?" Kathy asked.

"No, no one can stay. Just the patient," she said. She and the assistant began pulling feathers, bottles, and rattles out of the duffel bag. "Stand by the door and do not let anyone in under any circumstances."

We all began to file out when Linda called, "Kerry!"

I turned around. I smiled at her and nodded. "You'll be fine," I said.

"I want Kerry to stay! Please!" Linda said to the medicine woman, pointing at me.

The medicine woman walked over and looked me up and down, critically but not unkindly. "Okay," she said. "But you'll have to be strong. Can you do that?"

"Yes," I said, although I had no idea what she meant.

The assistant shut the door and they quickly finished unpacking. "You'll need to be protected," the medicine woman said to me. "Just stand over here, stay strong, and don't speak." She pointed to the other side of the room, far away from Linda.

Tears were rolling down Linda's face, and she had the look of a captured wild animal, desperate to escape and unable to move. Her eyes darted and her body trembled. Not knowing what else to do, and unable to embrace her or to say anything, I just looked at those big eyes of hers and tried to make her feel my love from across the room. Because, after all these months of getting to know Kathy and Linda, I had indeed come to love them very much. So I gave Linda the same kind of small smile I would have given my own frightened child, and I tried with all my might and all my imagination to send my love like a big wave of warmth flowing over her.

The medicine woman draped a heavy blanket over my shoulders and told me to hold it tightly around myself. She burned sage and waved it in front of me while she sang.

Then she turned to Linda in the bed and began. Linda looked more and more frightened. I smiled, I nodded. I tried to be that peaceful presence my book club friend had made fun of, because I didn't know what else to do. I tried the hardest I've ever tried to surround my patient in a bubble of love.

But I'll be honest. Eventually, I got bored. The ceremony was very long, and I was really hot. Sweat was dripping down my face and back and trickling down my legs into my shoes. I didn't understand what the medicine woman was singing because the words were in another language. Her movements were repetitive. My mind started to wander. After a while, I was no longer making a love bubble. I was making a grocery list.

Then suddenly, in a rush, I got very afraid. My heart started racing, my chest felt like it was being crushed, and all the nerve endings in my arms and legs went electric. It was as if a wave of dread and desperation had swooped in and rushed through and over me. I know it might sound nutty to describe emotion as having a physical trajectory, but it did. It went in through my feet and out my right shoulder and on up above me. It felt like being knocked over by a wave when you're walking out of the ocean.

It roused me out of my boredom for sure, and after I had caught my breath I went right back to trying to send Linda some love and reassurance. The singing went on for a few more minutes and then stopped.

"It's done," the medicine woman said quietly.

Linda looked stunned. "Is it gone?" she asked.

The medicine woman turned and faced her. "Yes. It's completely gone. It was very

powerful, and it was deeply, strongly attached to you. But it's gone now."

"I actually saw it," her assistant said. "It
was a black bird, maybe a raven or crow. It
flew out of Linda, down to the floor, and
then swooped up that way." She pointed to
the ceiling in the corner of the room. The
corner right above my right shoulder. Goose
bumps erupted all over me, and I felt like I
might faint.

The medicine woman came over and
pulled the blanket off me. I was drenched,
and the cool air felt good. More than an
hour had gone by. "You did well. You were
very strong."

She opened the door. Kathy was standing
there, waiting.

"Did it work? Is it gone?"

"Yes, it's gone."

"Will she get better now? Will the cancer . . ." Kathy trailed off.

"It doesn't work that way," said the medicine woman. "The spirit is gone, but the
damage remains."

Kathy began to cry, and she sank into a
chair in the hallway. But in just a few
seconds, she stood up, straightened her
back, roughly brushed the tears off her face,
and walked into the room.

"I'm so happy for you, sweetheart," she

said to Linda. "I bet you'll feel a lot better now."

"I already do," Linda said slowly.

Over the next couple of weeks, Linda continued to decline. If she was more at peace, I couldn't tell, because she hadn't seemed despondent before. Kathy continued to call from work, sobbing from the supply closet.

One day, Barb called. Before I could even say hello, she was yelling.

"Wait, Barb," I said. "Slow down! I can't understand you."

"She's lying! None of it is real. None of it!"

"Who?" I said.

"Linda! She made it all up. None of it is real!" Barb shouted.

Barb had finally tracked down Linda's next of kin, the estranged daughter, who, it turned out, was not all that estranged. She claimed that none of Linda's stories were real, and that there was not an ounce of Cherokee blood in her, let alone the blood of Wilma Mankiller.

Barb was on a tear. "That medicine woman came all that way for nothing! She gave us her time for nothing! I'm so embarrassed! Linda manipulated us! How could

she have fooled us all? She's a con artist!"
She paused for a second. "Wait," she said to
me. "Why aren't you upset?"

Barb was right. I wasn't upset by this
news. I wasn't even surprised. I had been
wondering about Linda's stories for a long
time. They seemed too remarkable, too
amazing. Impossible and unreal.

And yet. And yet.

The thing I had doubted most, had not
believed in, had simply dismissed out of
hand as impossible — Linda's evil spirit —
was the one thing I know for certain was
real. I had felt it myself.

I didn't know who or what to believe, what
was true and what was a lie, what was real
and what was not, at that point.

"But doesn't it bother you, not to know
what's real?" Barb asked. "How do you even
know what to believe anymore?"

Barb could not have known it, but those
two questions had been haunting me for
years at that point, ever since the psychosis.
How do you know what is real? And how
does anyone know what to believe?

Psychosis rips the firm ground out from
under your mind. It takes away your ability
to assess real from unreal. Even after years
of medication and weekly psychotherapy

had transformed me from a woman prone to dissociative blackouts and afraid to drive past hospitals and churches to one who moved in and out of both types of institutions easily, I still thought, sometimes obsessively, about the hallucinations and delusions I'd experienced. In what ways were they real? What could I or should I believe about them? They had really happened to me, after all. I'd really experienced them. Yet others had denied their reality and their impact on me. The questions of how you know what is real and how you know what to believe were familiar to me, and they troubled me.

Yet with Kathy and Linda, not knowing for certain what was true and what was fabricated, what was real and what was unreal, and not being able to discern what to believe about them, didn't bother me. Because in the midst of that cloud of unknowing, I could see something so powerful, so lovely, so real: that their love was transformative.

If you believe, as I do, that God is love, and not an old man in the sky hurling lightning bolts at unsuspecting innocents, and that this love is the creative force of the universe — and these are big ifs, I understand that — then you are, by the fact that you are created, loved. You are lovable because God loved you first.

But some people — maybe even most people — don't see themselves that way. Far too often, we've been taught not to see God that way. We've been taught the vindictive-old-man version of God, and not the creative-force-of-love version, and so we may never have known that we are lovable. Or perhaps, through the little dramas and big traumas of life, we've forgotten it.

When you don't know that you're lovable as you are, you need someone to show you. I don't think Kathy and Linda ever believed that they were lovable. Their childhoods were difficult, and their adulthoods terribly lonely until they found each other.

"I just can't believe that someone like that — someone like THAT — could love me," Kathy had said with wonder every time she spoke of Linda. "I don't really understand it. I don't understand how someone so amazing could love someone like me."

Once, she said, "If I never fall in love again, if no one ever loves me again, it will be okay. I can live the rest of my life just knowing she loved me. I'll know, no matter what happens, I must be okay because someone like Linda loved me. I'll live on that memory forever."

The astonishing thing to me, then and now, was that Kathy could not see that she was the amazing one. She could not see her own devotion, her patience, her advocacy, her strength, her passion. She could not see how lovable she was, until she was loved by Linda.

Linda, in the stories she had shared with Kathy, became the person she already really was — a person worthy of being loved and adored. That person — that fantastic, amazing, powerful, important woman who loved her — was exactly who Kathy needed, to show her how lovable she really was.

If Linda's stories were untrue as her daughter claimed, were they the effect of the brain tumor? Was she delirious or delusional, or even a little bit psychotic, as I had once been? Was Linda a con artist? A pathological liar? Or could it be that the overwhelming feeling of dread and fear I felt during her healing ceremony was how Linda had felt all the time, her whole life, and so she had concocted a persona who was strong and powerful enough to combat it?

I'm not condoning lies, or cultural appropriation of a group that has suffered oppression for centuries. But if she was lying, I'm trying to understand why Linda might have created another person to be.

Or was it all, in fact, true? Perhaps Linda had been telling the truth the whole time, and had simply never told her daughter about her real identity and her past. In my work, I'd seen people keep extraordinary secrets from their children, whether to try to protect them from the knowledge of the traumas they had endured or to protect themselves from having to reexperience them in the recounting. Could her daughter have simply not known? I don't know.

Here's what I do know for certain: I know I loved Linda and Kathy. I know I felt something terrible pass through me during the healing ceremony. I know the medicine woman believed that Linda needed that ceremony. I know that Linda died of brain cancer. I know that Kathy was by her side when she passed away. I know that Linda loved Kathy. I know that Kathy learned she was lovable because she was loved by such a remarkable person.

In the midst of unknowing, something absolute and real and true happened. Two women learned not just that they could love but that they were worthy of love.

ORDINARY ANGELS

"You'll never guess what," Anna said as she opened the front door. "I saw my angel in a patch of tar in the parking lot of Stop and Shop yesterday."

"Ahh," I said. Whenever I find myself in a situation where I have absolutely no idea what someone is talking about but the people around me seem to think I should, I give a long, heartfelt noncommittal *"ahh."* Usually, a good noncommittal *ahh* can buy you enough time to figure out what's going on, or at least which questions to ask.

Anna, however, wasn't buying the *ahh.*

"Well, you know about my angel, don't you? Do you not know?" she asked as she grabbed my elbow. She seemed shocked.

Smiling, pastel-colored ceramic angel figurines smiled down at us from all angles of the little living room, with its many comfortable recliners. There were pictures of angels all over the walls, too, brightly colored prints and posters. Some were in ornate gilded frames, most in simple black plastic frames from Target.

"Well, I suspected you really love angels," I said. "But, no, I'm not sure I know about your angel. Specifically. Your specific angel. You're saying you have a specific angel?"

"Oh." Anna sounded disappointed. "I just thought everyone knew." She looked away.

"Well, maybe I do know, and I just forgot. Sometimes that happens to me. You just need to refresh my memory."

"Because it's famous here in town. The newspaper even ran a story on me and my angel."

"Then I probably do know, somewhere deep in my brain. I forget so much. My mother used to say that I would forget my own head if it wasn't screwed on. Would you remind me?"

"All right. Just wait a minute."

Anna wasn't actually my patient. Her husband, Eddie, was. Eddie rarely talked. He always smiled briefly at me when I said hello and then ignored me, but he tracked his wife's every movement around the room. He adored her. I adored Anna, too, and my visits had really been with her. Now Eddie watched as Anna stood on the couch to reach a photo album at the top of a bookshelf crammed with more angels.

When she climbed down, Anna explained that she had an angel she saw all the time — at least once a month.

The freedom to believe people is one of the joys of being a chaplain. Other health care providers have to be suspicious by nature. Is she really taking her medication the way she's supposed to? Is she really following her diet? Did he really give up the cigarettes? Is he really staying home all day now that it's unsafe for his wife to be alone? But a chaplain is allowed to believe her patients. A chaplain may — no, *should* — believe the story of her patient's spiritual journey and what he thinks it all means, no matter where it leads.

But sometimes, I don't. I can't. Sometimes, I'm a skeptic. And in this case, it was even worse: I found Anna's belief cute.

Angels, of course — real angels as depicted in the Bible — are not cute. They are not pastel-colored. They are not babies. They do not even look angelic. The seraphim have four faces and six wings. The cherubim are eighteen feet tall and covered with eyeballs. The angels with flowing robes, streaming hair, and golden wings, the angels who play lutes and harps — these are not the angels of the Bible. While the New Testament's book of Revelation does mention angels playing trumpets, the blasts of those trumpets signal the destruction of the world. Not something you'd put on a Christmas card.

And yet.

Anna pulled a folded-up newspaper out of the album and opened it, turning the old pages carefully until she stopped and pointed to a photo. It was of the sky over the harbor at sunset. There, in the center of the gold and pink clouds stretching over the water, was the unmistakable image: a cloud angel. It flew on its belly. A long gown swooped around its ankles, its arms stretched forward, and it held a trumpet to its mouth. It was like something out of a potpourri-scented gift shop. It looked right at home among the statues and pictures in the living room.

"Do you see it?" she asked.

"Yes, clearly, absolutely," I said. "It's beautiful." And I meant it. But I didn't believe that the image was anything other than a remarkable cloud.

But then she opened the album. There, in one glossy developed-at-Walgreens four-by-six after another, was the same exact image of an angel. She'd seen him in clouds, in splotches of paint, in shadows, in the grain of wood, in bubblegum stuck to a picnic table. She had dozens of photos of him, flying on his belly and raising a trumpet to his mouth. It was delightful and alarming at the same time. I would not have believed it if I had not seen it, page after page after page.

"Do you see him here? And here? Now do you see why I call him my angel?"

There are lots of studies that show that people's brains are primed to see faces and patterns in inanimate objects. The phenomenon even has a name: *pareidolia.* We've come to understand that this predisposition became hardwired into human brains for survival. A baby who recognizes a human face or a hunter who sees patterns made by an animal in the grass is going to have an advantage over one who does not. The same natural tendency to look for and see faces and patterns all around us also sometimes inspires people to see the Virgin Mary in a piece of toast or an old man's face on the side of a mountain.

I don't know if pareidolia completely explains Anna's angel sightings. I do know, though, that angels are popular among hospice patients. Not with every one of them, of course, but with more than just a handful.

While Anna seemed content with her angel sightings and her thick photo album, another patient, Marjorie, approached the subject like a scholar. She dismissed the kind of angelology represented by kitschy figurines as "fluff," but for most of her adult life she had studied all that she could find on angels. She had read dozens of books and was writing her own book on the subject, she explained. She believed that every person has a guardian angel assigned to them at birth. You could get to know this angel if you learned to communicate with it. The angel could give you guidance and advice.

"How do you communicate with your guardian angel?" I asked.

Marjorie raised her eyebrows and crossed her arms over her chest. "How do I communicate with my angel, or how do you communicate with yours?" she asked. She always could see right through me.

"Both."

"How I talk to my angel and what I talk about with my angel is private," she said starchily. "But if you want to learn to communicate with yours, I'd suggest you start by asking him his name. That's just good manners."

"And he'll answer?"

"Yes, of course. That's good manners as well."

I wasn't sure if I was supposed to just talk to my angel in my mind, like a prayer, or if I had to say something out loud. But Marjorie seemed a bit annoyed by my questions, so I stopped talking and just listened to her plans for her book.

As soon as I got back out to my car after the visit, I sat down in the driver's seat and introduced myself to my guardian angel — out loud, just to cover all the bases. I asked my angel his or her name. Then I waited for a minute. Nothing happened.

I turned on the engine and headed off to my next patient.

A year or so later, my sister and I signed up for a beginner Reiki class. I'd first been introduced to Reiki at work, where several volunteers who offered it to the patients set up a one-day Reiki marathon in the office. Any employee could sign up for a twenty-minute introductory session. Developed in Japan in 1922, Reiki is based on the idea that there is healing energy in the world that can be directed and channeled by the laying on of hands. I didn't know how it worked, but I loved it. I felt so relaxed as the Reiki practitioner put her hands on my head and shoulders.

In the beginner class, we sat in folding chairs in a circle. The instructor asked all of us to close our eyes as she offered a guided meditation. Now, I love a good guided meditation, even the ones you can get on CD from the library or download for free on your phone. Usually they tell you to sit in a quiet place with your eyes closed and use your imagination to envision yourself lying in a meadow looking at the clouds, or hiking up a mountain, or floating in the ocean.

This meditation started in a similar way. The Reiki teacher had us envision ourselves walking through the woods and finding a cabin in a clearing in the trees. Open the door, she encouraged. Then she asked, "Do you see anyone or anything inside the cabin?"

To my surprise, I did. There was a couch with its back to the door and a plaid blanket thrown over the cushions. A golden glow seemed to be coming up from the couch. The glow sort of coalesced and turned into a young man with a shining, glowing face. He was beautiful and I couldn't stop staring at him.

"Hi there," he said, in my mind.

"Hi. Who are you?" I said back, still in my mind.

"I'm your guardian angel."

"Oh my God! I'm so glad I finally get to meet you!"

"Oh my God! I'm so glad you finally got to meet me! I've actually been here all along."

Was he making fun of me? Yes, I think he was. But I didn't care. Then I remembered what Marjorie had said. "What's your name?" I asked.

"David."

My eyes flew open.

Wait a minute, I thought. I'm just making all this up. This is all just my subconscious remembering what Marjorie said all those months ago. This isn't real at all. I'm just imagining this.

"No, I'm real," David said, loud as could be. "I'm really real."

I looked around the room. All the other students were sitting quietly, with their eyes closed. They didn't seem alarmed at all. They certainly didn't give any sign of having heard David's voice.

I did a quick inventory to see if I was going crazy again. I'd been doing these inventories for seven years at that point. It's a habit you develop if you've ever been psychotic. Even so many years later, I tended to question everything I thought and saw, especially if it was the least bit unusual. It was exhausting. I'd once shredded my Achilles tendon and had to wear one of those big immobilizing boots for months. When it came off, I'd been tentative and nervous in my movements for weeks. Just walking was nerve-racking, because I didn't trust my foot. This felt the same way, in the mind.

The last thing I needed was to think I'd met my guardian angel during a guided meditation.

I kept my eyes open for the rest of the class. David didn't seem to mind. "I'll still be here," his voice announced in my head.

Since then, David has shown up occasionally in my dreams, always with advice. "You're not supposed to plow through writing, or life," he said once. "You're supposed to let it fly." Another time, "God never calls you to do something without also giving you the ability to complete it." I always wake up flooded with relief.

Sometimes he tries for subtlety. This is always lost on me. Once, I was happily bouncing from rooftop to rooftop with a ninja in a kung fu movie-dream when I suddenly got scared. I refused to jump. The ninja yelled, "Just keep bouncing!" but I got angry. I stamped my foot, declared the whole thing ridiculous and demanded to know where we were going. The ninja morphed into David. "Jesus Christ, Kerry," he said, annoyed. "I was trying to show you that you don't have to know exactly where you're going to have fun getting there."

Once, he showed up as a very elderly man teaching a zumba class in a dream-gym. He came down off the stage where he was demonstrating the moves and stood in front of me, his flesh turning a sparkling gold as I watched. "You know," he said, "you're never going to lose weight when you're pregnant."

I had no symptoms at the time, but I woke up knowing I was pregnant. An over-the-counter test was positive. An ultrasound a few days later revealed that I had a rare type of ectopic pregnancy called a cervical pregnancy that, if not diagnosed and treated early enough, can rupture and kill the mother. If I hadn't had the dream, I wouldn't have had the ultrasound. It's strange to think that a dream could save your life.

So: Is David really my guardian angel? Is he a figment of my imagination, bubbling up from my dreams? Or is he a manifestation of my subconscious mind, my *animus,* in famed Swiss psychoanalyst Carl Jung's terminology? Does it matter?

Does it matter whether Anna's angel pictures were pareidolia or a real angel trying to comfort and strengthen her? Because that's what those sightings did for her. "My angel always appears to me just when I need him," she explained. "Whenever I think I just can't do it anymore, he shows up. Whenever I think I can't take it, he's there and I know I'm not alone. I know God loves me." Anna had no doubt that her angel was real, and she didn't care about other people's opinions of his reality. She knew that the comfort and encouragement and love he brought her was real too.

Is David real? Are angels real? Who gets to decide what's real and what is not? What does that word even mean?

When I was sick, the question of what was real and what was not real was all I could think about. Were my ketamine-fueled hallucinations of astral journeys real? After all, many indigenous tribes use psychotropic drugs to induce astral journeys, and the wisdom gained during those hallucinations is not just prized but believed to have a reality greater than the reality we generally inhabit. Thousands of years of Christian tradition have held mystical visions to be not only real but more real than this world, in which we see through a glass darkly. What I thought was God during my hallucinations insisted that it was the only thing that was real, and that it was this mundane "real world" that was an illusion. Anyone who has studied Eastern religions in even a cursory way is familiar with that idea. The belief in a reality beyond the reality we see and touch every day is a foundational idea of many belief systems.

But every single person I spoke to about the ketamine hallucinations told me they were not real. They were not a real religious experience. That was not a real encounter with God. There was no reality to them, and therefore no value.

When I was psychotic, I was absolutely convinced that the baby I'd been pregnant with had died, and I grieved as though I had had a stillbirth. In objective fact, my baby was alive and gurgling on my lap, but the nature of psychosis is such that a chubby, living and breathing infant is no refutation to a delusion. I sat on my couch and sobbed for hours, for months, over a dead baby. But while the grief was searing, debilitating, all encompassing, no one would acknowledge it was real. I felt the most alone I have felt, with my secret, deluded, inconsolable grief.

A year after my son was born, after I'd been on antipsychotics for about six months, a friend invited me to a luncheon gathering. I didn't know anyone else who was going so my friend sat me next to her sister, a psychologist. We got into conversation, and I told the sister that I had been diagnosed with postpartum psychosis. She was very sympathetic and kind until I explained that the psychosis had been caused by a drug.

"Oh, so you don't have real postpartum psychosis. My patients with real postpartum psychosis suffer so much. But yours isn't real."

It was a harsher echo of what so many loving friends had said to me when I told them about what I had thought, said, and done while I was psychotic: "That wasn't really you." But if it wasn't me, who was it? If it wasn't the real me, where had the real me gone?

When your ability to determine what is real is taken away by a drug, it's terrifying. But it's far worse when it's denied to you by other people.

Over years of listening to people's stories,

I've learned that many, many people — maybe even most people — will experience in their lifetime things that challenge their sense of what is real or possible. Three sisters ask their mother for a sign that she's okay after she dies. Each of them, separated by thousands of miles, opens up her mailbox the day after her death, and a butterfly flies out. A young man wakes up from surgery to find Saint Gerard sitting next to him. He has no connection to Saint Gerard, has never even heard of him before. He's told that it's an aftereffect of the anesthesia, but over the next six months until he dies, despite having no other neurological or psychiatric complications, Saint Gerard never leaves him. On a sunny day, three Pentecostal women pray over the husband of one of them. Just as the prayer reaches its crescendo, an enormous clap of thunder rattles the windows, and the wife faints. The TV weatherman that night cheerfully reports on an unusual weather occurrence that day, "a bolt from the blue."

Each of these incidents happened to people I knew. Anyone who works in hospice could tell you similar stories. They happen to many people, whether we embrace them or refuse to think about them, whether we are comforted or terrified by them.

True, such experiences can be explained by coincidence, by medicine, by meteorology. But the people who experienced them felt something more than coincidence.

When we dismiss an experience as "not real," what we are actually rejecting is the person's attempt at making meaning of the experience. That's a cruel thing to do. Attempting to find or make meaning is perhaps the central task of the spiritual life.

The single most helpful question anyone could have asked me when I was sick would have been "What does the experience you had on ketamine mean?" Nobody ever asked me that. It was dismissed as not "real," and therefore the meaning was not worth exploring.

How much more helpful, and kind — and enlightening — it is to ask what the meaning of the angels, the butterflies, the thunder, and the hallucination is.

Ellen's husband, Tom, answered the door and asked me in. Their house had that smell I think of as particular to the homes of the Greatest Generation. I've never been able to figure out what it is. Is it Pine-Sol or Lysol or Ivory soap? Is it the smell of decades of roast beef and mashed potatoes and buttered carrots seeping out of the walls? The house I grew up in in the 1970s and '80s didn't have it, nor does my house now, but the homes of both sets of grandparents did. What is that smell of warmth and cleanliness and safety? It smells more like home than my own home does to me.

Ellen's house had that comforting smell, but also the smell of sickness. That's a particular smell, too.

Tom explained that Ellen had enthusiastically requested a chaplain visit during the admissions interview, but he was dubious about what good the visit would do her. Ellen's long-term memory was fine, he explained, but she had no short-term memory, not even for conversations she'd had just five minutes before. "I'm not really sure what will happen when she meets you, or what good it'll do," he said. "She won't remember you the second you leave."

Still, Ellen seemed happy to have a visitor. I asked her about her days.

"You know what I do all day long as I lie here?" she said. "I try to be loveful."

I asked her what she meant.

"We shower so much love on babies and children," she said. "But as we grow up, it stops. No one showers love on grown-ups. But I think we need *more* love as we get older, not less. Life gets harder, not easier, but we stop loving each other so much, just when we need love most. I —" Her voice caught in her throat, but she took a big breath and kept going. "I need more love now that I'm so old. I need love."

She lay back on her pillows and closed her eyes, out of breath. In another few seconds, she opened her eyes again.

"One day, when I was lying here, I realized how old God is. He is so old. He must need so much love. People are always demanding so much from him, but who is there to shower him with love? So I thought that was something I could do. That's what I do all day: I try to love God. I lie here and try to make my heart burst with so much love. I can lie here and love God and maybe it will help him." She sighed heavily and her eyelids fluttered. She promptly fell asleep.

I sat there quietly for a minute, thinking. When I stood up, Ellen opened her eyes again.

"Why, hello there," she said with a wide smile.

"I'm so sorry, Ellen," I said. "I didn't mean to wake you up."

"That's all right. Who are you? Are you the nurse? Do you need something?"

"No, I, I . . ." It took me a moment to realize that she had no memory at all of our visit, or of me.

"I'm very tired," she said apologetically.

For the first and only time in my entire professional career, I knew exactly what to say.

"No, I don't need anything." I leaned over and put both my hands on her cheeks. "I just came by to tell you that I love you so much. And God loves you so much. You're surrounded by all the love you need." I leaned down and kissed her forehead, then lay my cheek on the top of her head, the way I'd done a thousand times with my children. "I love you."

Ellen grabbed my wrists and squeezed them. "Oh! I needed to hear that. How did you know? Who sent you? How did you know I needed to hear that? How . . ."

Her voice drifted off. She closed her eyes and fell asleep again.

The angels in the Bible aren't lute-playing babies, it's true. But most of them aren't multi-faced seraphim or eyeball-covered cherubim, either. Most angels in the Bible are messengers. They appear to people on earth looking just like ordinary young men but with messages of divine love and encouragement.

I don't know if Anna's angel was "real,"

however you define that term. I don't know if David is "real" in that way, either. I don't know what meaning Ellen may have made of a strange woman showing up in her room to tell her she was loved. I never saw her again. Likely she had no memory of it when she awakened.

I'm no angel. Nor am I saying or implying that any human is. But maybe the message — the message Ellen was putting out in the world as she lay there dying, the message that she'd unwittingly boomeranged back to herself, stayed with her. Certainly it's the only message I can consistently say is real, after all these years as a chaplain. Try to be loveful. It's the only message that makes a difference, and it does not matter from whence it comes.

IMAGINATION AND SUFFERING

Albert always sat in the same place — in a chair at the head of the bed, between Ada and the window. He alternated between looking into her eyes, holding a spoonful of melted ice cream to her lips, patting her sunken cheeks, and staring out the window. I always sat across from him, on the other side, his still-beautiful wife between us.

Ada was completely nonverbal when I met her, and her muscles were so painfully contracted that her fingers curled into themselves and clawed at the skin of her own palms. She had not moved in years, except to clench tighter and tighter into a ball. So it was her husband, Albert, that I got to know.

Every time I visited, Albert told the same story. He told it dozens of times. He told it the same exact way each time, using the same words and the same gestures.

"He loved those turkey feet. Oh, he

thought they were so funny. He pretended he was the turkey and we all laughed. He pretended to scratch me with them. But he was the one who got scratched."

Every time Albert told the story, he held his hands up in front of his face, hands taut and fingers half curled, like claws, like the talons of the turkey that his son had played with, the talons with which the boy had chased his father around and around the kitchen, the night before he died of meningitis on Thanksgiving Day. He was four years old. I can close my eyes and see Albert in front of me, making the same movements, over and over.

"His fever got so high, before we even knew it was happening. There was nothing they could do. All because we let him play with the turkey. He loved those turkeys. He used to laugh and laugh."

He stared into space, dumbfounded, mouth agape, and shook his head. Just as he did every time he finished the story.

Albert believed that the boy had gotten sick because he scratched himself with the turkey feet, and no nurse or doctor had ever been able to convince him otherwise. He knew it was meningitis, but he also knew it was the turkey feet. The turkey he'd raised and his wife had cleaned, the turkey they had let their son play with, because it made him laugh so hard.

Albert blamed himself. He should have known better.

"What can you do? What can you do? What can you do?" he repeated as he patted his wife's cheeks. It always ended this way.

When the story never changes — when someone tells the same story the same way, over and over, I get nervous as a chaplain. When my questions elicit no new answers, when my prayer seems to bring no comfort, when there are never new connections with other things the speaker has seen or learned or thought or experienced, when there is never any reflection about what happened, when the person does not even seem to know I'm there as he tells the story again and again, the same way each and every time — that means that the story is stuck, and the suffering is immobile. It means that there is no meaning to the loss. And if that loss is the story that defines your life, it can mean there is no meaning to life.

It might seem strange to think that grief has a life, but it does. It develops and grows, like an organism. Sometimes it undergoes a quick and startling metamorphosis. Empty sadness can turn into burning rage overnight. Stoic denial can crumble into hyperventilation in a moment. Sometimes grief changes slowly, almost imperceptibly, and one can see the changes only looking back twenty years, thirty years.

But one always hopes that it changes. When grief develops and grows, the suffering at the heart of it changes, too. It becomes less acute, less raw and fiery. I'm not sure it diminishes, but it somehow becomes diffused across the memories that surround the loss at the heart of it. It seems less concentrated, and therefore more bearable.

But some suffering seems frozen in time, like Ada, with her fingers clenched into claws that dig into her hands, and Albert, with his fingers clenched into claws that dig into the air.

"Everybody hates change," Rose declared, many years after I met Albert and Ada. "Nobody likes it. But I'll tell you the real truth: Change is a gift from God. We should get down on our knees and thank God every day that he made it so everything is always changing. That's how I look at it."

I had just told Rose that I'd no longer be visiting her because I was moving to South Carolina. I was sad to be leaving my friends and job and home. This wasn't the reaction

I was expecting.

"Everybody only thinks about the good things changing, that's the problem," Rose continued. "But if the good things didn't change, then neither would the bad things. And thank God the bad things change. No matter how bad something is, it'll change, too. We'd go crazy if nothing ever changed."

That boy in the hospital, who'd been shot and paralyzed from the neck down for his sneakers — the boy whose anguish I'd fled from, unable to make myself return — this is why he'd overwhelmed me so. I'd looked at him and his future and I could not see change. All I saw was a never-ending sameness. He would remain paralyzed. His unchanging words, repeated over and over again, drove home the point.

But the spiritual paralysis was mine. I looked only at his physical condition. I didn't consider that his spiritual and emotional life was not paralyzed like his body was. I didn't imagine the infinite ways someone with quadriplegia could lead a happy and meaning-filled life. I didn't imagine how I might create a sacred space in which he could grieve his losses, and in which his mind and soul could start to move beyond its present anguish.

My imagination failed him.

Rose's words are true, of course. Everything in this world changes eventually, though sometimes when we are in the midst of suffering we cannot imagine it.

When someone tells you the story of their suffering, they are probably still suffering in some way. No one else gets to decide what that suffering means, or if it has any meaning at all. And we sure as hell don't get to tell someone that God never gives anybody more than they can handle or that God has a plan. We do not get to cut off someone's suffering at the pass by telling them it has some greater purpose. Only they get to decide if that's true. All we can do is sit and listen to them tell their stories, if they want to tell them. And if they don't, we can sit with them in silence.

When people tell their stories again and again, turning them over and over, they're trying to make or find meaning in them. That meaning is something they have to discover for themselves. As painful as the process might be, there is no circumnavigating it, either with the most thoughtful ideas you can offer or with the most hackneyed clichés. The meaning a person finds will almost never be the same one you can come up with. It will always be richer, more nuanced, more surprising.

I had a patient once, a woman in her forties, who was dying of leukemia. She told me how she had prayed, so long and so hard. She wanted to get better, and she wanted to be able to mother her children again. Certainly she didn't want her children to grow up witnessing her pain. She had prayed and prayed, but she just got sicker and sicker, and the pain got worse and worse, no matter how much morphine she was on. Now death loomed, within weeks. She was going to die, and no matter how hard she prayed, nothing would change that. She had been despondent.

But on one of my visits, she told me with wonder, she'd realized that God actually was going to answer her prayers after all. "Everything fell away," she said, "and I understood, finally, that dying IS the answer."

I'm usually pretty good about keeping a calm demeanor with patients, but I could feel the shock cross my face. She smiled.

"Don't you see? Dying is what will take away the pain. It's the only way the pain is going to end, and the only way that my kids won't see me suffer anymore. You see what I mean? The only way the suffering is going to end is me dying. And I can teach my children how to die without fear. That's what they'll learn from me. That's how I'll be their mother." She paused, perhaps waiting for me to respond. I didn't know what to say.

"There's always a solution, I see that now," she said. "I just didn't understand it at first. It's not the solution I wanted. But there's always a solution. It's just not the one I assumed it would be."

She would teach her children how to die. That was the meaning and purpose she found in her illness and death.

I say it sometimes to my daughter, who feels things so deeply. "There's always a solution, sweetheart. You just haven't imagined it yet." I don't know why I say it, because it has never comforted her.

"You always say that, but in this case, THERE IS NOT!" she replies. I guess I want it to seep in somewhere deep in her subconscious, so that someday, when she is up against something truly awful, when the rug is pulled out from under her, some part of her will remember: that there is always a solution, that suffering is not forever, that some meaning can be found in even the direst of situations.

I also understand her knee-jerk reaction,

her instinctive rejection of that idea. It's a tough idea to swallow in the midst of suffering, maybe an impossible one even to contemplate. That's the nature of suffering — whether you are sufferer or witness, it makes it hard to imagine change.

But everything does change.

I'm not trying to glorify death, I'm really not. I'm just retelling the stories my patients wanted me to share, the ideas they had and the insights they gained, as best I can. I don't get to decide what those are. Some of them are strange and uncomfortable and even alienating when you first hear them. But as someone who has had the privilege of listening in on the insights of the dying, I can say that sometimes they are also radically liberating and breathtakingly creative. Patients find meaning in places where my own spiritual imagination fails me, meaning that is always so much more astonishing than anything I've imagined. That's why you have to let people find their own meaning: They will always do it far better than you.

But sometimes — sometimes — there is no meaning to find, no meaning to make. Sometimes in this world there is pain so great that all one can do is carry it. Carry it for a lifetime, with a story that never changes. Sometimes, there are just those absurd turkey feet, forever scratching the air.

In those cases, all that there is to be done is to listen. Sometimes, when I was over-tired, or had just come from another patient with a hard story, or just the way the story struck me that day, familiar though the story was, I couldn't keep my own tears in as Albert cried for his son who had died too soon, and for his wife who had lived too long.

I'd try to wipe the tears away surreptitiously, try to remind myself that the little boy he wept for was not my child, that Albert was not my grandfather. Usually this worked, because he was so absorbed in his grief. But he saw me once.

"Oh God, I made you cry." His voice cracked and broke.

"No, no, it's okay," I replied.

"Thank you for crying for my son. No one ever cries for him anymore, except me. And when I die, no one will cry for him ever again."

He paused and sighed heavily, all the air leaving his chest. "And maybe that will be a blessing. 'Cause we'll finally all be together. I won't need to cry no more."

Dying Is Just a Verb

"You know what I really want to do?" Betsy asked as I wheeled her down the hallway. She was in her eighties, widowed, and living in a nursing home. She had only recently, and unhappily, started using a wheelchair. "I really want to go outside and feel the wind in my pussy again. Could you help me with that?"

I just about lost it, right there in the hallway. When I stopped laughing, I said, "I don't think I'm allowed to do that. I think I might actually get in a lot of trouble if I pulled off your pants and wheeled you around outside half naked."

She sighed. "That's a shame. Probably because all the bigwigs in this place are men. They have no idea how good it feels."

That made me think: Had I ever felt that? Did I know how good that feels?

That night, I was at a get-together of other

mothers in the neighborhood. I was dying to tell that story, because, really, who wouldn't be? So after a few glasses of wine, I started in.

Until another woman interrupted me. "Oh my God, Kerry," she said, "I can't stand to hear stories about the dying! Stop! It's too depressing!" Some of the other women laughed, and agreed.

So I stopped, embarrassed.

Now, in this woman's defense, I'm pretty sure she was drunk, or on her way there. I don't think the other women meant to be mean. They were mostly stay-at-home mothers of very young children. I did that, too, for five years, and I know how difficult, all-consuming, and exhausting that work is. Being a stay-at-home mother was exponentially more emotionally, mentally, and physically draining than being a hospice chaplain could ever be. I think those women needed a night of laughter and freedom from responsibility. I think they thought whatever I was going to say would be a buzzkill on a rare night out.

How could I explain that while there are sad moments working in hospice, they're far outweighed by happy, enjoyable, boring, peaceful, frustrating, tedious, and yes, hilariously funny moments. These women were making the same mistake as the people who ask me earnestly, their voices hushed and their brows furrowed, "What is it like to work with the dying?" Both groups talk about and think about "the dying" as though they are some sort of exotic species. Both groups assume that "the dying" are different from the rest of us — people to be either especially feared or especially esteemed. This idea — that people who are dying are magical, wise, better, or, alternatively, terrifying, unearthly, macabre, is rampant. It's also not true.

The dying are just people, like you and me, who happen to be doing something we've never done. *To die* is a verb, like *to jump, to eat,* or *to laugh.* It's something people do, not who they are.

People don't somehow transform drastically into something else when they're dying. They're just doing something you haven't done yet.

I think of it sort of like sex. Remember back when you were a teenager, before you'd had sex for the first time? The mystery, the fascination, the ridiculous rumors? The fear? The sense that something about your very being would change when it finally happened?

Now it's just something you do, not who

you are.

Happy, healthy sex can be a powerful experience and expression of who you are, but it doesn't fundamentally change you.

Dying isn't going to change who you fundamentally are, either. If you were a hilarious, fun-loving, sex-in-a-meadow kind of person at thirty-five, you'll probably still be that way at eighty-five, even if you can't get your own pants off anymore. You might be even funnier, because you're no longer worrying as much what other people think.

If you were a selfish jerk in life, there's a good chance you'll still be a selfish jerk when you're dying. Dying doesn't automatically make you a better person. If you haven't asked for forgiveness or done any work to rebuild damaged relationships, reconciliation isn't going to magically come to you just because you're at death's door.

I was working in a hospital when I was called very late one night to do a bedside prayer service. The patient had had a massive stroke several days before and had never come back to full consciousness. The nurses believed that he was now close to death. His wife, his children and their spouses, and several grandchildren were all gathered around the bedside. He wasn't responding to anyone or anything anymore. I spoke briefly with his wife and asked her what she wanted from me.

She wanted a prayer. In these situations, I ask what the person who is dying is like — his family, his faith, his history, his personality — to try to incorporate some of that into what I say. Obviously I don't usually know the dying person, and I won't be able to get to know them at this point, but I use what the family tells me to try to say a prayer that will be at least a little bit personal and meaningful to everyone there.

In this case, the wife and kids talked about what a devoted father the man in the bed was, how he loved to take his children fishing, how he always made sure he went to their softball games and track meets and recitals. I incorporated all these details into my prayer, and together we commended him to God.

Afterward, the wife and kids told me how beautiful and meaningful they'd found that prayer. They thanked me profusely.

And I won't deny this — that felt great. It was an ego boost.

I left the family at the bedside and walked down the darkened hallway, feeling pretty good about myself. A man ran to catch up with me.

"Hey!" he called out. I stopped and waited

for him, and we walked together to the elevator. "I know they all loved your prayer, and you probably think he was a great guy," he said hoarsely. "But he wasn't. That's his second wife, and his second kids. I'm one of his first kids. I'm the only one of his first kids who's even here. The rest haven't talked to him in years. I just want you to know who he really is."

He stood there in the strange brown light of the hospital hallway at three in the morning, then continued. "He's a horrible man. He abandoned my mother and us when we were all little kids. Him and his mistress, that woman you met in there, moved all the way across the country and started a new life. New family, new kids, like we didn't exist. We saw him twice a year.

"How do you just leave your kids, and replace them with new ones? Yeah, I'm sure he was a great dad to them. He was a great dad to us — until he left. He's a shitty father, and your prayer was wrong, flat-out wrong. Fuck him. Fuck them. And fuck you, lady."

We continued to walk slowly toward the lights over the elevators at the end of the hallway. He stabbed the button for the lobby.

"I'm sorry my prayer hurt you," I said.

"Yeah. It didn't hurt me. I just want you to know the truth."

"I'm sorry your father abandoned you."

"Don't apologize for that. He did it, not you."

We waited.

"I'm sorry I said, 'Fuck you,' " he said.

"It's okay," I said. "I messed up."

"Yeah," he said.

The elevator car arrived and we got on.

"You know what I wanted?" he asked. "I just wanted an apology. I just wanted him to look at me and say, 'I'm sorry.' That's it. I didn't get it."

The doors opened. He waited for me to get out first. I turned to him and said, "Can I get you a cup of coffee? We could talk for a minute if you want."

"Nah. There's nothing here I want," he said. He walked out of the elevator, through the lobby, and into the darkness.

If the dying don't somehow transform into especially wise, mystical, and magical people, neither do the people who take care of them.

Caregivers are not on the whole kinder, stronger, more patient, or more loving than the rest of us. They are not special, and despite what all too many people tell them, they do not feel blessed by God to have been put in the situation they're in. Or at least, none of them has ever said that to me. Many felt abandoned. Most just didn't want the job — not because they didn't want to take care of their spouse, parent, or child, but because they didn't want their spouse, parent, or child to be dying in the first place.

The popular insistence that caregivers to the dying are living saints is connected to the belief that the dying are different from you and me. And it does real harm.

A husband whose wife was bedbound for more than ten years with multiple sclerosis told me that sometimes he saw the women who used to be his wife's friends in the grocery store or at church. They earnestly squeezed his hands and wanted him to know that they were praying for her.

"She doesn't need your fucking prayers!" he exploded. "She needs you to visit! Don't make God your fucking patsy because you don't want to come!"

People who are taking care of the dying are doing exhausting work — exhausting physically, emotionally, mentally, and spiritually. They're doing it with only as much strength and energy and the same needs and weaknesses as they had before the bottom fell out and their life was turned upside down by a terminal diagnosis in the family. Pretending that they have superhuman strength means that all too often, we're allowing them to go it alone. It deprives them of the help they need, it deprives the dying of the comfort and companionship they need; and it deprives us, as well, of an understanding we very much need: that nothing — not even death — effortlessly takes away our weaknesses or magically transforms us into who we want to be.

Someone once asked me if I thought people should plan what their dying words will be in advance. The short answer is: No. Whatever last words you say, there's a good chance you're probably not even going to be aware that they're your last words while you're saying them. That Hollywood death, where people whisper secrets or words of great wisdom right before breathing their last, doesn't happen. Most people either fall unconscious for days before they die or die too suddenly to speak. Or they are too weak or confused to speak meaningfully, or they say last words that are expressions of surprise, like "Look!" or "Oh my goodness!"

The longer answer is: Why would you do that? If you had something so important to tell your loved ones that you're taking the time to plan it out, why in the world wouldn't you say that important thing right now? This very moment?

If you want to apologize, then apologize now. If you want to tell someone you're proud of them, say it right now. If you want to express your love, call up and say, "I love you." If you want to ask for forgiveness, do it this second, while there is still time to do the actual work that's involved in seeking and granting forgiveness and arriving at some reconciliation. Don't hold back.

Those things might be difficult, even frightening, now, but dying won't make you courageous. Dying doesn't make you someone else. If you can't find the strength while eating, walking, or vacuuming the living room, it seems foolish to think that you'll find the strength while doing an entirely new activity.

That's not to say that enormous change and growth can't happen in the last months, weeks, and even days of life. It does. I've seen it.

But I've also seen the work that goes into such changes. It's the same work that change requires when one is healthy, when one isn't learning how to do something new.

If there is any great difference between the

people who know they are dying and the rest of us, it's this: They know they're running out of time. They have more motivation to do the things they want to do and to become the person they want to become, up until the very last breath. But you don't have to wait until you're dying to do that. There's nothing stopping you from acting with the same urgency the dying feel.

If you want to be someone who knows what the wind feels like on your skin when you stand outside naked, do it now, while you can still pull down your own pants. Do it now, so that you can remember what it feels like when you can't do it anymore.

Become who you want to be while you can enjoy it. Don't put off doing the work of becoming who you want to be. Waiting will not make it easier, and time is short.

It's a Beautiful Life
and Then You Leave It

"Whatever you do, don't let Millie stay in the room when they take the body out," Peggy, the hospice nurse, whispered. She held a piece of paper to her cheek, to shield the family from hearing what she was saying. "She does not need to see that." We were sitting on the overstuffed sectional sofa that ringed the living room amid a dozen of Anthony and Millie's relatives. Anthony's hospital bed, and his body, sat in the middle, where I imagined a coffee table once sat.

Anthony and Millie lived on the top floor of that peculiarly New England style of building called a triple-decker. Built a hundred years ago for the working class and the poor, triple-deckers consist of three identical apartments stacked atop one another, with a narrow winding staircase leading to each. The landing outside the apartment door was a cramped area less than three feet wide.

I had just pulled into Friendly's for dinner and ice cream with my children and husband when Peggy called. It was my birthday, but I was also the chaplain on call that week. I hadn't met Anthony yet, but now he was actively dying, and the family wanted a prayer.

I drove straight over from the restaurant, but by the time I got there Anthony had already died. It must have just happened, because Peggy was still listening for his breath and heartbeat, still feeling for a pulse, when I walked into the dark and low-ceilinged apartment.

Once Peggy went through all the steps of the examination and quietly pronounced his death, the family started telling stories about Anthony's life. He and Millie had met when they were teenagers. They'd been married more than sixty years. They'd lived in that apartment for their entire married life and raised five children there. When Peggy finished with Anthony's body and pulled the sheet up and over him, neatly folding it down over his chest and tucking in the sides, as though tucking a young child into bed, she sat with us, too, and we waited for the undertaker to come.

It was when those somber men in baggy black suits knocked on the door that Peggy whispered her plea.

The family, Peggy, the men from the funeral home, and I gathered around Anthony's body in the living room and said a prayer. Then Peggy hugged Millie, said good-bye, and left. The female relatives headed to the kitchen to clean the pots and put away the uneaten dinner they had brought a few hours ago. The men went outside. The funeral home men went downstairs to get a gurney and a body bag from the hearse.

That left Millie and me, and Anthony, in the living room.

"Why don't we go in the kitchen?" I said to Millie.

"No," she said. "I don't want to leave Anthony."

The funeral home men came back upstairs.

Many people are very skinny when they die; Anthony was naturally heavyset and now hugely swollen with fluid. The men set up the gurney next to his bed, unfolded the body bag, and opened it. They slid a board under his body. On the count of three, they heaved the board on top of the body bag on the stretcher. It landed with a thud.

"Why don't we go downstairs and get some fresh air?" I said to Millie.

"No," she replied, continuing to stare at her husband.

The men carefully tucked Anthony's limbs into the bag and zipped it closed. Then they tightened four straps around his body to fasten him to the stretcher.

"Why don't we sit in the bedroom while the men finish getting Anthony ready to go to the funeral home?"

"No."

The two men looked at me and furrowed their brows. One gave me a barely perceptible shake of his head. The other darted his eyes from Millie to the kitchen door, back to her, and to the door again.

"Millie, I really think we should leave the room now. These men are going to take very good care of Anthony, and I think it would be upsetting to watch him leave the house," I said.

"I want to stay here."

A look of panic flashed across the younger man's face. "We'll take good care of him, ma'am," his older partner said.

"That's fine. But I'm going to see him out."

"It's not going to be easy, Millie," I said.

"I understand," she said.

The two men grimaced ever so slightly at each other and set their lips in a firm line.

Then they wheeled the stretcher to the door.

Anthony's body had not been strapped to the stretcher, as it first appeared to be. Instead, the straps simply encircled the body bag. They cinched Anthony to the board inside the bag. At the landing, the men lifted the board up and off the gurney, one of them at each end. Then they slowly tipped the board until it was completely upright, as though Anthony were standing up in his body bag. His head flopped forward, making a protrusion in the vinyl fabric. With one man in front, facing the body as though they were dancing, and the other behind, they shook and shimmied Anthony's body to get it out the door and onto the landing.

Any dead body is heavy — dead weight — and Anthony's was heavier than most. The two men from the funeral home struggled, though they tried to hide it. They grew breathless and called directions to each other in barely controlled grunts as they tilted and turned the upright board to try to maneuver it and themselves through the low doorway and onto the staircase.

I stood next to Millie as she watched them. As they started to walk down the stairs, they managed to get her husband's body back into a horizontal position. But before the man at the top was even out of view, the man at the bottom called out to him to tip the board up again and to the right, to try to get around the first of the many turns in the stairs.

We heard bangs and scrapes, the men grunting and shouting to each other, as respectfully as they could, to *hold him up!* or *wait wait wait!* all the way down the three flights of stairs. At one point, we heard a boom and a clattering that suggested one or both of them had lost his grip on the board altogether.

I cringed, wondering what to say. Before I could think of anything, though, Millie sighed and grabbed my hand. "It's okay," she said, still staring at the open door her husband had just gone through for the last time.

When we finally heard the downstairs door slam, Millie walked over to the window and watched as they put Anthony's body in the back of the hearse. "It's a beautiful life and then you leave it," she said. I'm not sure if she was talking to her husband, me, or herself. Maybe she was talking to God.

Pink cherry blossom petals blew off the stunted tree in the median between the sidewalk and street and floated around the three men. She turned to me with shoulders slumped and threw her hands out to the side.

"What now?"

I've heard people say — usually in an attempt to comfort or motivate others, or sometimes to stifle their grieving — that loss, tragedy, trauma don't define you.

That, of course, is utter bullshit.

Anyone who has been through a great loss or a terrible trauma already knows that the experience defines you. If there is one truth that runs through my patients' stories, it's that. At the very end of their lives, they defined themselves by the stories they chose to tell, of the hard things they had been through.

But in watching how their stories developed — how they reflected on and reassessed and made new connections between those losses and other events of their lives — it had become clear to me that if those hard things define us, it was equally true that each of us gets to decide exactly how they define us. We get to decide what the definition is. We get to decide what it means.

Is your life one of regret or hope? Does it have to be one or the other? Is your body the locus of trauma, or a source of joy? Can it be both at the same time? Can you find kindness toward yourself and others amid your pain and anger and fear? Is there something real in all the facades and personas we create, or in the mysteries we encounter? Can life be both beautiful and crushing at the same moment?

When I was in orientation for my first job in hospice, the chaplain training me encouraged me to write down in the visit notes whatever lovely things patients said, even if it was just a phrase. Even if no one ever read those notes (and I'm certain almost no one ever has), the patients' hopes and ideas and thoughts would still exist, and would not be lost, she explained.

So when I sat down the next day to write up the visit from the night before, I started to write what Millie had said. *It's a beautiful life and . . .*

I put my pen down. That couldn't be right, what with the utterly awful way the funeral home had had to remove her beloved husband's body. She must have said, "It's a beautiful life *but* then you leave it," I thought. I crossed out the "and" and finished the quote.

I looked at what I had written. No, no. No, that wasn't right, either. I distinctly remembered the "and" because even in the moment it had startled me. Yet the next day it seemed impossible.

I usually write a note for a visit right after the visit has finished, but I hadn't this time. I'd wanted to get back to Friendly's to join my children for dessert. And now, the next day, I was no longer sure what Millie had said. How could I have forgotten so quickly what had struck me as so poignant just half a day before?

I think it's because it's startling every time — every single time — that such beauty and such loss coincide in every life, in every soul, in every memory. It doesn't have to be that life is beautiful *but* it must end. It can be that life is beautiful . . . and still, as much as we may not want it to be so, it ends. It can be both beautiful and, by the very truth that it ends, full of loss and tragedy and trauma. The two can coincide. They do coincide.

Here's how I now think about what happened to me when my first child was born: I still don't understand what happened. I don't know why it happened. I still don't know what was real and what was hallucination, but I know with certainty that it has value. It has meaning. It created who I am today. If there's one thing my patients have taught me, it's that the concept of real and unreal is not as black and white as I once thought, because this life is not as black and white as I once thought. I've learned that it's far more interesting and ultimately peaceful to live in the space between. I've learned that my burning shame did not blot out love. I learned that I could lose my mind, my identity, my ability to function, and yet still be someone. I learned that the best thing to alleviate the suffering of the soul is the kindness of another human being. I learned that there is more mystery in the world than anyone taught me when I was growing up. My life veered off on a path I had never imagined on a hot Iowa Blooms-day when a thunderstorm blew through, and yet I don't regret it. I wouldn't wish it on the Devil, but I don't regret it, because everything I hoped for was there among the pain and terror. It's the path that led me to work in hospice, in large part because I was afraid of death and illness and wanted to see what was on the other side of that loss. What I found were the patients who healed me. They were all so broken, and so beautiful.

If life were like a novel, and I could tie things up nicely with a bow, I would claim that it was Gloria who gave me my parting advice. But it wasn't. It was a little old Jewish lady who gave me a blessing every time we met. She'd fled Poland with her parents and brother in the 1930s and arrived in the United States ten years later alone. A woman whose story I haven't told here, and will instead keep bundled in my heart with the hundreds of other stories. I'll leave you with it, as she left it with me: "Promise yourself," she said that last time we met, "promise that you'll have a great life, no matter what happens."

ACKNOWLEDGMENTS

I'm so thankful to all the patients and families who let me into their lives, whether for a year or for ten minutes. I have loved every one of you, and my hope is that it shows in these pages. I will always be grateful.

It's an honor to have worked with some of the best chaplains, nurses, aides, social workers, doctors, and volunteer coordinators I've ever met. Thank you to all of you for teaching me how to work with people at the end of their lives, and for the unfailing support you've shared at difficult times and with heartbreaking cases. One of the best parts of working in hospice is getting to work with other people who work in hospice. Thank you.

If you had told me ten years ago that I would ever write another book, I would have laughed. There's no way to fully express my gratitude to Bernie Vaccaro and Tziporah

Cohen for helping me get better.

So many people helped me with this book, and in so many ways. My deepest thanks to all of you, and especially Becky Saletan, Marly Rusoff, Katie Freeman, Claire McGinnis, Ben Denzer (that cover!), Michelle Koufopoulos, the entire staff of Aspen Words, Isa Catto Shaw, Daniel Shaw, Chrysti Shain, Mary Egan, Kristin Egan, Kit McIntyre, Kristin Miles, Colette Sartor, and Tricia Escobedo.

And finally, thank you to my husband, Alex Ruskell, and my children. I couldn't have written this book without you, and I wrote it for you.

The employees of Thorndike Press hope you have enjoyed this Large Print book. All our Thorndike, Wheeler, and Kennebec Large Print titles are designed for easy reading, and all our books are made to last. Other Thorndike Press Large Print books are available at your library, through selected bookstores, or directly from us.

For information about titles, please call:
  (800) 223-1244

or visit our Web site at:
  http://gale.cengage.com/thorndike

To share your comments, please write:
  Publisher
  Thorndike Press
  10 Water St., Suite 310
  Waterville, ME 04901